The Lifer and the Lawyer

The Lifer and the Lawyer

A Story of Punishment, Penitence, and Privilege

BY
George Critchlow
WITH
Michael Anderson

CASCADE *Books* • Eugene, Oregon

THE LIFER AND THE LAWYER
A Story of Punishment, Penitence, and Privilege

Copyright © 2020 George Critchlow. All rights reserved. Except for brief quotations in critical publications or reviews, no part of this book may be reproduced in any manner without prior written permission from the publisher. Write: Permissions, Wipf and Stock Publishers, 199 W. 8th Ave., Suite 3, Eugene, OR 97401.

Cascade Books
An Imprint of Wipf and Stock Publishers
199 W. 8th Ave., Suite 3
Eugene, OR 97401

www.wipfandstock.com

PAPERBACK ISBN: 978-1-7252-7837-0
HARDCOVER ISBN: 978-1-7252-7836-3
EBOOK ISBN: 978-1-7252-7838-7

Cataloguing-in-Publication data:

Names: Critchlow, George, author. | Anderson, Michael, coauthor.

Title: The lifer and the lawyer : a story of punishment, penitence, and privilege / by George Critchlow with Michael Anderson.

Description: Eugene, OR: Cascade Books, 2020

Identifiers: ISBN 978-1-7252-7837-0 (paperback) | ISBN 978-1-7252-7836-3 (hardcover) | ISBN 978-1-7252-7838-7 (ebook)

Subjects: LCSH: Anderson, Michael. | Lawyers—Biography. | Criminal justice, Administration of—United States.

Classification: KF373.5743 .C8 2020 (print) | KF373.5743 (ebook)

Manufactured in the U.S.A.   12/07/20

Author's note:

This book is based on a true story. It portrays real people and real experiences. Certain scenes and dialogue have been written to recreate the spirit and feel of events and conversations whose detail is long since lost to memory. In some instances, in order to maintain their anonymity, certain names, characteristics, and locations have been changed.

To Michael for his inspiration; to my wife, Diane, for her support; and to both for their patience.

I have wrestled with the angel and I am
stained with light and I have no shame.

—Mary Oliver

Contents

Prologue | 1

Part 1: Retribution and Redemption | 3
Part 2: Darkness | 45
Part 3: (White) Privilege | 84
Part 4: Due Process and Equal Protection | 94
Part 5: The Great Mandala (Wheel of Life) | 151
Part 6: Empathy and Faith | 169

Epilogue | 189
Postscript | 201

Prologue

Chains bound my client's feet to his hands and neck. He stood at counsel table, immobile, bent and sad, dressed in a bright yellow jumpsuit, surrounded by a small police force and a mob of reporters anxious to scribble the final words of a terrifying drama. An indignant judge would soon sentence him, a judge who hated his violence, his audacity, and the color of his skin. The judge believed Michael to be depraved and irredeemable, and almost everyone agreed. They wanted him to die in prison.

The sentencing was a long time ago and it is strange to think that it occurred before I had lived most of my life. Now, I am nearing old age, looking back more than ahead. My client, too, is getting old—a great-grandfather, a committed, longtime man of God, and still behind bars after forty-two years, even though he has killed no one and has been a law-abiding, model prisoner for three decades. His name is Michael Anderson and he inspired me to write this book.

Anderson has spent almost 16,000 days in a prison cell where he is officially known as Prisoner #287309. I have spent the same time practicing law, teaching law, and exploring the world. The irony is that I believe he has traveled further than I, and his reach—his potential for impacting lives, for doing good—is greater than mine. I am not envious because I would never have wanted to trade places. But I look at him with wonder, I respect him, and he has become my friend.

As a child, Michael never once heard anyone tell him "I love you." For him, this is very much a story about emerging into the light out of a dark background, a story about trauma, redemption, transcendence, and learning how to love. For me, a product of privilege, the tale of our connected lives raises questions about how we become who we are. Is it our nature or is it determined by the conditions to which we are born? Can we change who we are by an act of will? And what is the role of faith? For forty years, I wondered about the consequence of our different skin colors and family histories. Most significantly, I questioned whether Michael's spiritual and moral metamorphoses came from correctional coercion, inborn will, or divine influence.

We imagine our paths are freely chosen. But there is a need to account for biology and history, the random intercession of other people, culture, race, and the mystery of the transcendent. The variables make it difficult to predict the course of any individual life even though there are those who claim expertise in such matters.

This book is a collaborative account of my long journey with my old client, and what we have learned: about the effects of childhood trauma, the importance of communicating love, the pernicious effects of racism, the purpose of punishment, and the redemptive power of faith and self-knowledge.

Part 1: Retribution and Redemption

Chapter 1

"Ring the bells that still can ring, forget your perfect offering, there is a crack in everything, that's how the light gets in . . ."

—Leonard Cohen

The Franklin County Courthouse is a stately example of Renaissance Revival architecture that oddly materialized not in Florence or Rome, but in rural railroad towns of the American West. The edifice was built in 1913 after Pasco became the county seat of Franklin County and county commissioners decided to construct a public building whose appearance might conjure a world beyond the wind and dust of eastern Washington.

The courthouse boasted two Ionic columns that supported a portico and roof. These buttressed a magnificent rotunda, the interior of which was accented in gold and inlaid with cream colored marble. If you could stand on the top of the rotunda, you could see where the Columbia River joins the Snake River at today's Sacagawea State Park, the place where Lewis and Clark camped on their way to the Pacific eleven decades before the courthouse was built.

The weight of the building created its own gravity. Regardless of the distractions occasioned by the day's client or case, when called to the courthouse I was always mindful of the marble and gold, the great dome's encompassing girth, and the palpable irony of such a structure's existence in this provincial corner of the world. The formal elegance was not without comfort, but it occurred to me that the nature of the place produced in some people an inflated sense of self-importance.

I walked through the courthouse's massive front door on a bright September morning in 1979 knowing this would be the last time I saw my client outside prison walls. My brain churned with professional calculations and

I was fully engaged in my role as a partisan lawyer. But I was dispirited by an uneasy feeling that I was David without so much as a slingshot, and Goliath would soon have his way. I climbed the circular staircase to a packed second-floor courtroom. People stood or sat wherever they could find space. In time, Judge Knight's entrance was announced, and he ascended to his accustomed position. The man's considerable physical stature complemented and enhanced his judicial prestige and he commanded the courtroom the way General Patton commanded the Third Army.

The judge shuffled some papers, adjusted his glasses, and looked down from the Superior Court bench at the man who stood before him in yellow prison garb and chains. This was followed by a long pause as the judge shifted his focus to the assembled people squeezed together on rows of courtroom benches: sheriff's deputies, city police officers, victims and their families, courthouse regulars. He then turned to the right, to the jury box now reserved for the press, and his gaze lingered for a moment on the squirming collection of reporters and newscasters. He nodded, almost imperceptibly.

I stood at counsel table with my co-counsel, Tim Mahoney, our client standing between us. The courtroom was quiet, all eyes on the arresting black-robed man flanked by Lady Justice and the American flag. Behind him hung the great seal of the State of Washington. It was a setting designed both to inspire and intimidate. The judge ignored Mahoney and me and turned to the defendant.

"Mr. Anderson, are you prepared to be sentenced?"

I answered on his behalf. "We are, your honor."

Judge Knight shot me an impatient look and turned back to my client.

"You have the right of allocution. You are probably not familiar with the term. It means that you have the right to say something on your own behalf before I pronounce sentence. Do you have anything to add to your lawyers' plea for lenience at last week's hearing?"

The defendant understood his right to allocution well enough as we had discussed it in private just that morning. He had no desire to address the court.

Again, I spoke for him: "Mr. Anderson does not wish to address the court, your honor."

My words provoked the judge. "I am not talking to you, Mr. Critchlow," he scolded. "I'll let you know when I want to hear from you."

PART 1: RETRIBUTION AND REDEMPTION

"With all due respect, judge, Mr. Mahoney and I are here representing our client. We are ethically bound to speak for him if he chooses not to speak for himself."

A week earlier Mahoney and I had argued that our client's serious crimes should not deprive him of a chance to someday rejoin his family and reenter society. I had urged the court to take a close and sympathetic look at the defendant's background, especially the neglect and abuse he suffered as a child. Tim reminded the court that our client had committed violent crimes but had not killed anyone. Convicted murderers were often given a realistic chance for parole, and so should Anderson. We conceded he should not be released without evidence of rehabilitation, but we urged the court to structure a sentence that would allow at least a possibility for parole before the defendant was a doddering old man. The judge then delayed sentencing for an additional week while he reviewed the court record and the recommendations of experts.

Now, I was not optimistic. Judge Knight continued to ignore me. He fixed his eyes on the defendant like a hunter zeroing in on a wild beast. I stood before him vibrating with the memory of what the judge had said a few months earlier behind closed doors, in chambers, during the course of an intensely combative trial. While debating technical legal points relating to Anderson taking the witness stand, the judge had struggled to compose himself. He was overcome by the dark part of his being that was supposed to be vanquished by education, discipline, and the rule of law. He might be given credit for his candor, but the words he excreted were profoundly unseemly and astonishing to the mind of a young lawyer who believed even the most conflicted judge would overcome or conceal his prejudice.

"I am going to get that black S.O.B. whether you put him on the stand or not," Judge Knight had said to me. "This discussion is over!"

It was time for that promise to be fulfilled.

Judge Knight announced: "Very well, I shall sentence you forthwith, Mr. Anderson. You are perhaps the most notorious criminal ever to be prosecuted in Franklin County. You are the most dangerous man I have ever had the misfortune to encounter. Your life is a recipe for how to inflict suffering, terrorize communities, take what is not yours, and forsake the most basic obligations that make for a decent society. I will delineate the acts and events that make up the horror story that is your regrettable life. Before doing so, I want you and the world to know that I intend to impose a sentence that will insure, as much as is possible under our laws, that you spend the rest of your life in prison and that you never again walk the streets of this or any other community."

The judge continued but the point was already well made. Justice had been rendered. A brutish interloper from a distant inner-city jungle would never again threaten the decent folks who lived on the quiet banks of the Columbia River in southeastern Washington.

* * * *

For months, the local *Tri-City Herald* newspaper had entertained its readers with courtroom photographs of Michael Anderson's handsome black face. Some photos showed his lean, sinuous body bent by chains that shackled his feet to his hands as he stood before different judges to answer for violence and wrongdoing. The paper reported that Anderson was the "only person in the state, perhaps the nation, to face ten consecutive life terms, two concurrent life terms, plus another forty years."

Under Washington law, a parole board determined a convicted felon's actual release date, if any. In the case of a life sentence, or multiple consecutive life sentences, as in this case, the parole board could decide that the defendant should never be released. The board's decision would ultimately be based on many factors, including the recommendation of prosecutors, sentencing judges, and victims.

Here is what Benton County Superior Court Judge Frederick said in 1978 when sentencing Anderson to his first bundle of consecutive life sentences:

"My goal is you be kept literally in prison for the rest of your natural life."

The *Tri-City Herald* agreed. It's editorial at the time was titled: "Throw Away the Key" and applauded the court for rejecting Anderson's "pathetic" plea that his sentence should reflect the fact he had not committed the ultimate crime—murder. The newspaper said:

"Give him another chance . . . and the odds are high he will kill someone."

After being convicted and sentenced on the second batch of Franklin County charges in 1979, the case in which I was involved, all five Franklin County prosecutors signed off on a seven-page written recommendation to the superintendent of the Washington Corrections Center. The concluding sentence was unambiguous:

PART 1: RETRIBUTION AND REDEMPTION

"The below signed staff of the Franklin County Prosecutor's Office recommend that Michael Anderson spend the remainder of his natural life behind bars."

Judge Parsons and Judge Knight added handwritten postscripts to the prosecutors' recommendation. Judge Parsons said, simply:

"I concur with Prosecutor."

Judge Knight wrote:

"I specifically concur that Michael Anderson never be paroled. He should spend the rest of his life in a controlled environment."

A court stenographer who sat through one of the criminal trials went out of her way to record her belief that Anderson was a monster who should be locked away forever. Probation officers, crime victims, and the public agreed.

In the eyes of the court and court-watchers in 1979, Michael Anderson would always be a dangerous, fierce-looking, twenty-five-year-old black man in chains, a man who should never be given another chance to do harm. There was no inclination or capacity to imagine an alternative picture: of Michael Anderson at age thirty or forty or fifty or sixty; of Michael Anderson praying in his cell; of Michael Anderson tending to the sick and dying; or of Michael Anderson engaged in years of hard work confronting the trauma of his own childhood as well as the trauma and injury he had inflicted on others. In time, Michael Anderson was mostly forgotten. Those few people who remembered him at all, and those responsible for determining how long he should remain in prison, pictured him as he was in 1979.

A short ride back to the penitentiary marked the end of Michael's youth and the end of courtroom appearances. For all intents and purposes, it also marked an end to personal autonomy for the rest of his life. Chained and alone, he rode in the same sheriff's van that had shadowed him since he first prowled the streets of Pasco the previous year. He could not see far but what he could see looked like a long and brutal gauntlet that led to old age and death.

* * * *

For me, as a young lawyer, the Michael Anderson case was exciting because it was high-profile, stimulating because of the legal challenges, and professionally rewarding because of what I learned. Nevertheless, the experience deflated me. I was happy only to have it over. I was most unhappy with the fact that all our work had resulted in a real possibility that Michael would die in prison.

I was troubled by the notion that a person could be considered irredeemable. I was not a neuroscientist or psychologist. Law school didn't teach me much about criminology or the behavioral sciences. Still, to my mind, no one, including a judge, could definitively predict a young man's destiny, or his potential for transformation. Who could forswear the possible triumph of a man's battle to overcome his demons, his desire to heal, to move from brokenness to grace? Maybe it was my inherent optimism, or the influence of the Enlightenment, or my years of exposure to the Episcopal liturgy. I did not believe people were all bad or all good. I believed in human perfectibility and had a hard time accepting a court's desire to condemn a young man to lifelong imprisonment.

Of course, it could be that the courts and the experts knew more than I about the prospects for rehabilitating a violent criminal who was regarded by many as a psychopath. Everyone knew psychopaths could not be fixed. But Michael was not a psychopath. He was not Ted Bundy or Charles Manson. He had what is described as an antisocial personality disorder. If I had known what scientists would later find out about criminal behavior through brain imaging, neuroplasticity, and more sophisticated diagnostic tools, I might have presented the court with evidence that certain parts of Michael's brain were indeed working, parts that did not work in the brain of a psychopath. These are the parts that allow a person to feel guilt and remorse. They enable people to draw moral conclusions about their antisocial behavior even though they find it difficult to stop the behavior. Unlike psychopaths, whose underdeveloped brains prevent them from feeling, the antisocial personality arises from environmental conditions and is treatable.

I might also have educated myself and the court about the likelihood that Anderson suffered the adult consequences of Reactive Attachment Disorder (RAD)—a disorder caused by an infant's inability to form healthy attachments to parents and caregivers. The science and understanding of how the brain responds to early childhood trauma has accelerated in recent decades. There is a developing scientific consensus that the nervous system responds to trauma by creating neural responses that protect a traumatized individual from unsafe conditions even when those conditions no longer exist. A child who is neglected, abused, shamed, and rejected may, for example, grow into adulthood with a nervous system built to help an infant survive constant stress and fear. That adult may flee, fight, act out, become numb, dissociate, manipulate, or seek comfort through addictive or aggressive behaviors because the child's brain is wired to respond in certain ways to certain stimuli. What we know today, in 2020, is that the world is filled with people haunted by trauma, people who are not fully present, who make unhealthy decisions, and who pursue behaviors unconsciously intended to fix or defend against something distressing or painful that may have occurred long ago.

Fortunately, the brain is pliable, and the effects of traumatic events can be counteracted by new environmental stimuli and a variety of therapeutic approaches. The point is this: it is true that some people are very damaged. It is not true that they are all unsalvageable. And it is neither wise, economical, nor humane to assume that a twenty-five-year-old will be the same person at age sixty.

To put it in a Christian context, one that is relevant to Michael's story, shouldn't New Testament values counteract Old Testament justice?

Chapter 2

"Prison is a second by second assault on the soul, a day to day degradation of the self, an oppressive steel and brick umbrella that transforms seconds into hours and hours into days..."

—Mumia Abu-Jamal

Michael was now Prisoner #287309 and he would spend many years at the Washington State Penitentiary before correctional authorities trusted him enough to move him to a less secure facility. His adjustment to life in the prison would have been more challenging and severe had he not spent his youth preparing for it. He had been in and out of juvenile detention and jail since he was eleven and had previously been incarcerated for almost four years in the Illinois State Penitentiary at Joliet. The Illinois penitentiary had been no cakewalk, but Michael's physical prowess, his reputation, and his street sense had enabled him to work his way up the inmate power structure. He was young, but not a newcomer, not a new "fish," in prison parlance, and he befriended older inmates who ran drugs and other contraband, managed prostitution, and controlled the tactical decisions involved in inmate race relations.

No one knew him at the Washington penitentiary in Walla Walla when he first arrived. But his reputation preceded him. Inmates watched the news and were familiar with Michael's eastern Washington crime spree and his criminal history in Illinois. Not only that, inmates immediately started calling him "Iron Mike" even though he had not mentioned his Illinois nickname. Iron Mike had already become a legend of sorts. The legend was mostly based on false or exaggerated stories. On one occasion, he had supposedly beaten up five police officers who tried to arrest him. Another famous myth described the time when Michael, after being taken into custody, became so angry and aggressive he started salivating and used his teeth to tear off his handcuffs. While his reputation may have deterred some inmates from challenging him, other inmates and many prison guards targeted Michael precisely because of it. Like a notorious quick draw in the

PART 1: RETRIBUTION AND REDEMPTION

Old West, Michael was sought out by young guns and correction officials who wanted to prove themselves.

The Washington State Penitentiary was reputed to be among the worst prisons in the country, certainly the least desirable place to spend time in the Washington correctional system. It was known for assaults, rapes, murders, riots, lockdowns, violent inmates, and an impotent prison staff. It was the designated venue for execution of death row inmates by hanging. Michael knew he was destined to go there when he was screened at Shelton, the western Washington facility where psychologists and counselors determined that the most dangerous inmates would be locked up in the most dangerous and unforgiving of all prison venues—the penitentiary's maximum-security unit. Michael remembers the six-hour ride from Shelton to Walla Walla in the Gray Goose, the armored van that shuttled new prisoners to their assigned homes in prisons throughout the state. Shackled together on metal benches, the anxious men feigned nonchalance as they expelled gas that collected in the unvented space to a degree that the men's arrival at the penitentiary was a temporal deliverance as well as a descent into hell.

It was a hellhole run by the condemned. Every new inmate had to find his own cell or be assigned to a segregated setting. That's the way it worked in a society that was mostly managed by other inmates through the RGC—the Resident Government Council—which controlled everything from cell assignments to prostitution and ice cream concessions. Fortunately, Michael had made advance arrangements through prisoners at Shelton to reserve a cell. Within a month, he had his own cell, 6 Wing F-4. Cells were prime real estate bought and sold for value. The price in dollars, goods, or sexual services was a function of the value you placed on the location of your five-by-ten-foot cement cubicle—the place you might live for years, or for the rest of your life.

He was at the prison only a few hours when he was on his way to the mess hall and witnessed a prisoner almost kill another prisoner with guards looking on. When he asked why the guards had not intervened to stop the fight, he was told that guards don't do that at the Washington penitentiary.

In previous decades, the prison was a "super custody" facility where the warden exercised absolute authority. One word, and a prisoner could be standing naked for months in an empty cell or sent to the mental health ward where he might be tortured using coercive therapies, including electroshock treatment. Change began in the early 1970s with well-meaning but naïve reform. Inmates were given extensive new freedoms and governing power. Chaos descended. Convicts had the only keys to certain prison areas. They had access to prison offices and telephones. Bikers roared choppers around the Big Yard. Marijuana was everywhere, and hundreds shot heroin. Convicts took lives with shanks and even bombs. Frustrated and afraid, correctional officers quit or were paid by inmates to look the other way.

All of this meant that Michael had to earn his respect the hard way. He was not especially worried. Survival was what he knew. Plus, he was angry and had little to lose. He quickly discerned who to talk to, who to hurt, and who to befriend. The power dynamic from prison to prison was the same. Tough guys, guys with clout on the outside, and risk-takers ran the show. Tough guys who were smart had the most leverage. Iron Mike was both savvy and dangerous.

He started planning an escape, something that had possessed him at virtually every institution in which he had been incarcerated. There was the escape in the dead of winter from the small county jail in Illinois when he sawed through metal bars with a hacksaw smuggled in by a cellmate's girlfriend. There had been the two-day breakout from the St. Charles Boys' Home when he was fifteen. A few years later, Cook County authorities had charged him with attempted escape and assault when he tried to take a jail guard hostage after threatening him with a shard of glass. His more recent escape from the Franklin County Jail was well known to penitentiary staff who were especially vigilant in watching Michael for any signs of an escape plan.

Prisoners had escaped from the maximum-security unit at the Washington penitentiary. They dug tunnels, built ladders, paid off prison guards. They were almost always caught. Michael was involved in one escape attempt that was aborted after he had crawled halfway through a finished tunnel and heard a gunshot coming from the other end. A fellow inmate had been shot when he exited the tunnel and tried to run. The prison administration reinforced the message he had already gotten from inmates. You could fight, take drugs, maybe even kill—but the behavior had to be confined to the inside of the prison. You could not escape. When Michael accepted that escape was not a realistic option, he decided to become a player in the prison culture. He would become a king in this jungle where he expected to spend the rest of his life.

The ability to wield power and be perceived as powerful was easily established when the Lifers' Club designated Michael as "facilitator" of the

PART 1: RETRIBUTION AND REDEMPTION

Club's "ways and means committee," meaning he had responsibility for collecting unpaid debts owed to the Club by inmates who had borrowed funds to buy everything from candy, magazines, and tobacco to drugs and protection. Iron Mike had become the center of discussion as cons debated how tough he was when he made the rounds collecting for the committee. He was afforded a late-night pass that gave him access to all the prison cell blocks. The cons might avoid him during the day but there was no hiding once they were locked down for the night. Michael would quietly enter the cell block, locate the con's cell, and engage the individual in a quiet discussion about the consequence of defaulting on contractual obligations. The message was communicated in a way that could not be misunderstood. Michael occasionally had to employ force to collect debts that were seriously delinquent. The amount of force was dependent on the nature of the debt, the degree of resistance exhibited by the debtor, and the message the Lifers' Club wanted to send. Any doubts about Iron Mike's previous reputation were dispelled when Michael demonstrated the power and ferocity that had dominated his life since childhood.

It was not long before Michael was tested by a con for whom violence was a daily and gratuitous way of life. He was regarded as among the most unforgiving and brutal men in the maximum-security unit. "Blood" was his name and he was a tall, big-boned man with a notorious knockout punch that generally ended a fight quickly and efficiently. In addition to random violence, he had a record of fifteen wins to zero losses in bare knuckle fights organized informally by the Lifers' Club. No one wanted to fight him, including Michael. The two had engaged in a friendly commercial transaction when Michael first came to the penitentiary and the deal had presumably provided a foundation for continued goodwill. Blood had sold Michael a beautiful handmade quilt. However, he threatened to take it back after inexplicably claiming that Michael had not paid him the agreed compensation.

The ensuing fight took place among dozens of other cons congregated in the prison yard. It was not what Blood expected. Michael struck first, knocking Blood to the ground. Blood got up bleeding profusely from the nose and mouth. The full force of Blood's signature punch then found its mark and Michael was momentarily staggered as he fought to keep his legs under him. He recovered and came back at Blood with a barrage that put Blood back on the ground. Blood got up and produced a "shank," a homemade knife, with which he managed to stab Michael in the thigh while targeting his stomach. Wounded and bleeding, Michael wrestled for the knife and successfully pulled it from his leg. He propped himself with his good leg and faced his adversary with steely, unblinking eyes. Michael was ferocious now, consumed with rage, fearless, single-minded, and pitiless. His fists were fast and furious, stopping only when Blood lay on the ground bleeding and unconscious.

Michael had validated his reputation. Word got around. Other inmates began to gravitate towards him with overtures of friendship and alliance. They did not want him as a foe. The ever-watchful prison staff started giving Michael a measure of latitude he had not previously enjoyed. All of this reinforced the negative behavior that had troubled Michael since childhood. He could now be manipulative, intimidating, and selfish with minimal resistance.

* * * *

One day followed the next, each filled with anxiety and intrigue about matters ranging from the trivial, like negotiating for a small quantity of marijuana, to the existential, such as fending off a random attack by a dangerous sociopath. When he was not preoccupied with scheming or worrying about the unexpected, Michael faced soul-destroying boredom, a convict's most relentless and ubiquitous antagonist. There was nothing gentle in this world, nothing soft or heartwarming or blissful. Michael was not expecting to feel happy—ever. The most he could hope for was a measure of physical security. He had such moments, usually when he lost himself in the mindless repetition of prison labor, or when he was alone in his cell.

When Michael relaxed and let his guard down, let his mind wander, he would think of his girlfriend, Dee, and his two children. They were only forty miles away. It was logistically and financially difficult for Dee to visit, but she finagled and sacrificed and begged to obtain transportation for regular trips from Pasco to Walla Walla. The visits, however, were limited in number and duration. Because Michael was a lifer, the prospect of getting a time cut did not motivate him to stay out of trouble. However, he tried to avoid behavior that might result in a loss of visitation privileges. At some level, he recognized that his connection to his family was crucial to his survival, even as he berated himself for being a complete disaster as a father and partner.

There was talk of inaugurating a new program of conjugal visits for married inmates. Michael wondered if Dee would have him as her husband.

Chapter 3

*"Faith is taking the first step even when you
don't see the whole staircase."*

—Martin Luther King Jr.

By 1990, Michael had spent well over a decade in constant war with prison officials, other inmates, and himself. His unceasing conflict and many life sentences produced such a fatalistic outlook that each depressing day was like the day before and the next, dismal days unbroken by moments of hope or positive growth. His pessimism was an oppressive weight that blocked any uplifting thought or emotion. For several years, Michael numbed himself by shooting heroin, a substance easily obtained in the penitentiary in the 1980s. When not using heroin, he managed his pain the same way he had throughout his youth—by acting out aggressively against those around him. The only respite was periodic conjugal visits with Dee, now his wife, and his son and daughter. And age. The passing of time slowly eroded the impulse to rebel and fight. There was a gradual calming but no fresh insight and no hope.

No one was seriously injured in the 1989 Washington State Penitentiary riot. The ostensible purpose of the riot was to achieve better conditions for maximum security inmates. But, like most forbidden activities, it was also about the excitement of disruption and the personal pleasure derived from challenging correctional authorities. In any event, the consequence for Michael was segregation for several months even though he had not instigated the riot.

The cell was bare. There was a toilet in the corner, a metal bed, thin mattress, a blanket, and nothing else—no reading or writing material, no news, no communication with other prisoners except for yelling from cell to cell within the tier. Michael was now thirty-eight years old, worn out, and more despondent than he had ever been. His life was either the hell of segregation or the lesser hell of monotonous days, repetitive work, watching his back, and waiting, endless waiting, for what?

He was older now, less violent and less impetuous, but still hollow. He imagined the sole purpose of his life was to experience punishment. Some might argue it was Dante's Contrapasso—the place in hell assigned in proportion to one's sins. However, the punishment was not measured only, or even predominately, by the wretchedness of each day. The real measure was the fact those days would only end in death. And then Michael would have to deal with the small matter of eternity.

Ministers were always coming by to talk to prisoners and encourage them to turn to the Lord. Some were nonsectarian and easy-going. Others were dogmatic Bible thumpers. Michael was always tolerant, but skeptical. He was open to religious conversion as a Christian because his mother was Christian, his wife was Christian, and he assumed that God, should he ever present himself, would be a Christian God. But, as much as he had hoped and prayed for some kind of divine intervention, even before he was in the Washington State Penitentiary, God had never presented himself, never made himself palpable and accessible, never manifested in the form of some indisputable and undeniable force. Michael figured either it was all a hoax, or that he was, in fact, the irredeemable person almost everyone thought him to be—so irredeemably off the charts that even God had written him off.

He was in segregation when a minister, Ralph Thompson, came by his cell. It was January 19, 1990. The minister did not say much, and what he did say was oddly uncomplicated. It changed Michael's life forever. The minister simply inquired if Michael had tried to embrace Yahweh, explaining that Yahweh was the ancient Hebrew term for "the Lord." Michael answered, honestly, that he had but nothing seemed to work for him—not his prayers or his vigilant efforts to observe God's presence. The minister asked Michael if they might grasp hands for a moment. Michael said yes and the two men reached for one another through the bars and clutched one another's hands. The minister looked Michael in the eyes and said, "All you have to do is believe. Just believe."

The minister smiled and excused himself to continue his work. Michael stayed still for a moment and then heard another voice, disembodied and remote. It came from somewhere on the tier.

"Just believe."

Just believe. It was an epiphany. Michael was ready, had been ready since he had sensed God's presence almost fifteen years before when he was consumed by a powerful lament in Illinois' Harvey City jail. He had never imagined that belief alone could conjure God's presence without some additional requirement in the form of extreme penance or evidence of a miracle. He had looked for and insisted on proof that God was truly God.

Now Michael considered another approach. He spent the next several hours wondering if it could be that easy. Just believe.

That night he prayed and did nothing more than express his belief in a higher power. He asked nothing and made no commitments. The next morning, he decided to go the entire day without swearing or taking the Lord's name in vain. It was easy. The following day he did the same. In the evening he prayed and expressed his belief. Day by day, he reaffirmed his belief, and adopted different behaviors and different ways of relating to people in the prison community—inmates and prison staff alike. He decided not to disparage people. He decided not to scare or threaten them. In time, he decided not to hurt people. Instead, he looked for other ways to resolve conflict and mitigate anger. He also decided to get along with prison guards. It took time but not too much time. Michael gradually shed his reputation as someone who could hurt you. He slowly became known as a person who could be counted on to defuse potentially violent confrontations.

He looked different to himself when he looked in a mirror. When he got out of bed in the morning he felt lighter. Other inmates noticed and remarked on the change. Dee was elated. Michael's conversion inspired her to double down on her own faith. They started praying together when she visited. Their struggles became less stressful. His mother came to visit from Chicago and was overcome, exclaiming that the troubled look he had had since he was young was gone. She started crying and praising God for answering her prayers.

The prison chaplain soon gave Michael a job as custodian of the chapel. He also gave him a Bible. Michael discovered a nascent capacity for discipline and patience. He started paying attention to his own and other peoples' feelings. In contrast to his history of self-loathing and his pursuit of selfish, passing pleasures, he found that each day presented a new and different opportunity to feel good about himself in a lasting way. Michael's regular Bible studies commenced at this time and he fell in love with the book of Psalms. Twenty-eight years later, he continues his studies and is steeped in knowledge of the Psalms as a guide to prayer, praise of God, and pious living.

Michael Anderson's last prison infraction for many years occurred on May 28, 1991, just over one year after his meeting with the minister, and fourteen years after entering the Washington State Penitentiary. Prior to 1991, he had sixty-eight major infractions ranging from assault, attempted escape, possession of drugs, possession of weapons, disobedience, disorderly conduct, and rioting. His only major infraction in the last twenty-seven years occurred in 2006 at a different prison when, ironically, he argued with a prison chaplain about his upcoming baptism and was cited for not leaving the chaplain's office promptly enough after being told to do so.

This man who committed crimes and hurt people from age ten in 1963 to age thirty-seven in 1990, suddenly changed—fundamentally, convincingly, and enduringly.

Chapter 4

"None who have always been free can understand the terrible fascinating power of the hope of freedom to those who are not free."

—Pearl S. Buck

Before his evangelical experience, Michael had been surprised when Larry Kincheloe, the penitentiary superintendent, took a special interest in him. Kincheloe managed the prison during the mid to late 1980s, a critical time of transition from prisoner control of the penitentiary to control by corrections officials. He exercised power with integrity and humility. He raised staff morale but also invested in relationship-building with inmates. Michael's relationship with staff at that time was not good. When Kincheloe reached out to Michael, he did so not because it was a routine part of his job but because he recognized something in Michael beyond his reputation as a tough guy. Kincheloe visited Michael on multiple occasions. He spent time with Michael and Dee together. He called Michael his friend. The two men stayed in touch even after Kincheloe left the prison in 1988 to become statewide director of prisons. On Kincheloe's order in 1989, Michael was transferred from the penitentiary's maximum to medium security unit. Michael promptly squandered the opportunity when he tested positive for cocaine use and was returned to maximum security. Nonetheless, he was profoundly impacted by the fact that the state director of prisons had expressed faith in him.

On August 29, 1990, after Michael gave his life to Christ, I wrote Kincheloe to communicate what, in my opinion, was an extraordinary transformation in Michael's attitude and conduct. I asked Kincheloe to submit a supportive statement to the parole board on Michael's behalf. The letter concluded with the following comments: "For what it's worth, my own contact in the last year with Michael reveals an enormously changed individual who demonstrates maturity, thoughtfulness, and awareness about the consequences and morality of choices one makes in life. If rehabilitation is still one of the goals of our system of criminal justice, Michael is a remarkable example of success."

I later spoke with Kincheloe in 1991 concerning his view of Michael's prospect for eventual parole. He expressed his belief that Michael's sentence was unrealistic and that he should work toward eventual release. He believed in Michael's ability to check his more destructive tendencies and he was convinced Michael could be as strongly pro-social in the future as he was antisocial in the past. Kincheloe followed up this conversation with a letter to the Washington Parole Board that said: "I can only emphasize once again that [Michael] is making a tremendous effort to adhere to policies of the institution and the department . . . His counselor reports he constantly strives to maintain his positive behavior and to control his aggressive behavior." When Kincheloe, a retired military officer, left his position as director of prisons at the end of 1991, he wrote Michael a letter in which he said, "I wish I could have known you in different circumstances. You would have been a hell of a soldier and would have done well in many other careers."

Over several years, Kincheloe's message to Michael, in person and in writing, was that Michael's time structure—his sentence—was excessive. He encouraged Michael to have hope, to believe that there was light at the end of the tunnel, to have faith that the parole board would someday release him. He reminded Michael that he, Michael, could influence his own destiny—he could choose to conduct himself in a way that advanced his opportunity for parole, or he could live in such a way as to block the possibility. Coming from the prison superintendent and later director of prisons, this message caused Michael, for the first time, to think of the long term, to envision his life over the decades, to imagine his middle age and his old age. This implanted something new in the inmate who had always felt hopeless. A new vision evolved, a vision of living a long, fruitful life and the possibility of release, however remote.

The parole board met with Michael on December 19, 1990. The meeting convened in the penitentiary's administrative wing in a room that would have been utterly bare but for the single table and five chairs. Michael's counselor was there, there was a pro bono attorney from the local prison legal services office, two board members, and Michael. One of the board members was an older man named George Johnson. He entered into a dialogue with Michael about his crime victims. Everything about Johnson's message—his demeanor, his countenance, his choice of words—revealed to Michael that the parole board official was a remarkably empathetic and dedicated man. He cared about the people Michael had hurt, but he also cared about Michael. At one point during the hearing, Johnson got up from his side of the table, walked over to Michael, leaned down, and whispered, "How could you do this, son? How could you betray your humanity?" Michael's response was involuntary and unexpected. He felt years of repressed pain gather in his abdomen and he doubled over as a great cramp seized his gut and tears flowed from his eyes. He slid out of his chair onto his knees in an eruption of physical and emotional pain. A moment later he fully collapsed on the floor, writhing in agony, crying uncontrollably, his lawyer, counselor, and board members staring in wide-eyed alarm. In time, Michael composed himself and went to the bathroom before returning to the meeting to thank the board members. Something had happened. He left the hearing feeling liberated, lighter, and more transparent. He could tell that something new, something good was at work inside the dark and inscrutable part of his being that had seemed always to be in control. He was now walking toward the light.

Once he accepted God into his life, Michael immediately began receiving the benefit of small miracles—"gold nuggets," he calls them—that he perceived to be tangible proof of God's love and that acted as a stimulus for strengthening his faith. One such incident happened in 1991 when Dee and Michael's two-year-old granddaughter, their first grandchild, was diagnosed with a serious vision problem. An eye surgeon in Pasco wanted to operate, but some inarticulable apprehension caused Michael to say no. A penitentiary official known for his harsh treatment of prisoners inexplicably offered Michael the name of another eye surgeon in Spokane. The Spokane surgeon ultimately performed the surgery, which completely restored the granddaughter to normal vision. Michael and Dee later discovered the original surgeon had been the target of several medical malpractice claims.

Perhaps the biggest nugget among Michael's many blessings was the fact that his faith validated him in the eyes of his children. They became increasingly grateful to him as he grew in his ability to emotionally support and inspire the family. He began, awkwardly and haltingly, to reach out. His heart warmed in ways that were unknown to the old Michael. A softness was introduced to his world of metal and brick and he experienced the power of humility and compassion. Iron Mike was learning how to love.

* * * *

And that is the essence of the story. Not my story—for I am still seeking proof of God's presence—but Michael's story. The narrative continues because there are matters of consequence yet to be told and because some might wish to know if Michael's transformation was truly lasting and authentic. Of interest also is the question of whether he ever gets out of prison. And you may ask at this juncture: what is there to be learned for those of us who care about human behavior, spiritual formation, and criminal justice? Is rehabilitation for the supposed incorrigible just a matter of random religious inspiration? Should we simply put more ministers in the prisons? Or is Michael Anderson's life instructive in other ways?

Michael's religious understanding is different from my own and that difference has created both tension and richness in our developing relationship. He can accurately be described as an evangelical Christian. My religious orientation is born of New Age psychology, Eastern mysticism, an Episcopal family tradition, and an affection for the fabled moral teachings of Jesus Christ. This is admittedly a spongy foundation as compared to a belief system based on supposedly inerrant doctrine, but it allows for appreciation and affirmation of things that resonate deeply, including the mystical and beautiful, things that may suggest the path we are on even when that path is otherwise indecipherable. It may be similar to the way we are drawn to different kinds of music.

I listen to Bach's beautiful, Christ-inspired masses and passions. I also love Chopin, although history teaches he was not a man of God. I hear curious and ethereal world music emerging from Islamic traditions in the Middle East. My continuing affection for the Beatles is partly due to the group's exposure to Hindu religious philosophy that inspired them to send a message of love to millions of young people. Leonard Cohen's songs and poetry reflect the irony and tension that inheres in the study of Buddhism. They help me better understand moral ambiguity and dark and light sides of love. More recently, I have become enamored of Josh Groban because his music is gorgeous, melodic, and fulsome without requiring any explicit call to faith.

I am unwilling to label myself by reference to a continuum of religious and philosophical beliefs. I cannot say clearly that I am an atheist or agnostic or believer. I am open and closed at once. My journey with Michael Anderson bears witness to my sense that our redemption, in life and beyond, does not come with a label—and our capacity for friendship and understanding transcends difference and doubt.

Chapter 5

"At their peak, religion and psychotherapy become one."
—Maryanne Williamson

Michael's life in the penitentiary dragged from year to year but not from infraction to infraction or fight to fight. His orientation had changed, and he now focused on prayer, work, education, and relationships rather than scheming, aggression, and assorted prison dramas. He had spent years watching men dive off high prison tiers to their death because they could not tolerate prison or their own dark psyches. He had seen men hang themselves, slash their wrists, and set themselves on fire to escape darkness and end suffering. There were drug overdoses, beatings, murders, and mutilations. He, himself, had been stabbed in the leg during the fight with Blood, the inmate who wanted to kill him. His goal now was to use spiritual and emotional growth to transform the all-encompassing horror that defined life in the penitentiary.

After a few years of working in the prison chapel under the watchful eye of the chaplain, Michael began intensive one-on-one psychotherapy with a prison-contracted community mental health counselor. For the first time in his life, he began peeling and understanding the imbedded layers of defenses and excuses he had used to justify his earlier lifestyle and choices. For over two years, weekly therapy sessions yielded insights and surprises that allowed him to slowly comprehend the person he had been. His goal was not to kill that person, but to heal him and integrate him into a new life guided by Yahweh and dedicated to righteousness. It was not easy. He worked through childhood pain, self-loathing, feelings of emptiness, guilt, and anger. The therapist made him look at his criminal conduct in light of his feelings about his mother, his stepfather, and his absent biological father. He learned to talk about how it felt to be emotionally and physically unsafe as a child. Michael explored and began to understand the relationship between sexuality and power that had dominated his attitude toward women. Much of the talk therapy dealt with the difficulty Michael had in empathizing with another person's needs and pain.

Even before he began therapy, a 1994 comprehensive psychological report noted that Michael "appears to have matured emotionally and has improved impulse control." The psychologist was impressed with the cessation of infractions and the fact that "unlike other inmates, [Michael] has maintained continued contact with his wife and family members." That same year, the prison administration showed its support and confidence by giving him a job as a clerk in the prison retail store where Michael routinely handled thousands of dollars in cash transactions and prison script.

A May 1996 report from his mental health therapist documented Michael's positive and noteworthy response to individual therapy:

> At both the intellectual, insightful and at an affective, gut-level, he appears to have much better understanding that the abuses and neglects he suffered as a child and his suppression of his hurts and angers about them provided the fuel for his criminal and destructive acting out behaviors. . . . Clearly, through all his acting out and criminal behavior and through his disruptive behaviors in the penitentiary through much of the 1980s, Mr. Anderson was not consciously aware of the repressed defiance and rage left in him as a result of the abuse he suffered as a child. . . . With therapy, he appears to have a much better understanding of the sources and depth of his angers and his energies and how to turn stressful situations into prosocial and individually self-enhancing situations rather than into a clash of enemies wherein both he and his perceived adversaries were bound to lose. . . . Prior to and independent of his therapy with me, Mr. Anderson appears to have developed an intrapersonal structure, including religion and goals and morals' restructuring that has allowed him to redirect his life, at least within the prison environment, in an impressive and prosocial direction.

By 1996, Michael had not only finished two years of mental health therapy, he had a GED, two Associate of Arts degrees, one in general studies and one in custodial services, and a successful history of work in the prison chapel, gym, and retail store. A psychiatric evaluation submitted in April 1996 in connection with an upcoming parole hearing stated: "At this point, Mr. Anderson appears to be doing all anyone asks or expects of him." The parole board congratulated him on his progress and encouraged him to keep it up. More importantly, the board changed Michael's earliest possible parole eligibility date from 2057 to 2025. He was now convinced that his past challenges and future salvation were things within his control. In the past, he had battled people, but the battle was not with people, it was within. The Lord showed him that everything he needed to be successful was already in him and had been since he was in his mother's womb.

* * * *

What did Michael's progress mean on the ground, where it counted, with other inmates and staff in a culture where guardedness, aggression, and emotional remoteness were the currency of interpersonal relations? How does a prisoner transition to thoughts and conduct that are empathetic and sincere? Once one begins to value the Golden Rule, how is it implemented in practice?

One strategy is simply to avoid discordant situations whose gravity pulls one back into a chaotic world of impulses, fear, vengeance, and violence. Another is to establish goals and the discipline to achieve those goals. The goals might involve education, religion, work, reading, therapy, physical fitness, art, or any creative process that introduces new ways of thinking about oneself and other people. Some inmates change their lives through daily meditation or prayer. Still another approach is learning how to communicate and interact with other inmates and staff in an intentionally supportive way, one that builds positive relationships and signals potential friendship. The key is to unlock the inmate's creativity so that he is no longer defined by his crime or entrapped by his former thoughts.

Michael remembers one morning sometime in the mid-1990s. His world had been spiritually and mentally expanded but, outside of increasingly faint memories, his relationship with the physical world shrank to match the dimensions and configuration of the Washington State Penitentiary. There was definition and predictability to almost everything. The mind-numbing routine was now less onerous after decades of repetition and conditioning. Michael had adapted the way a caged zoo animal adapts to the confines of prescribed space. His world had become worn and familiar. Still, there were always choices.

On this morning, he became aware of something unusual. A white guy in another cell on the same tier had slit his wrists to the bone and was laying on his bed trying to die. Ray was a schoolteacher from Spokane doing time for a domestic murder. He decided to be done with prison life, but his chosen method to leave the world was not instantaneous. Blood oozed from his wrists and was absorbed by the mattress. When guards came around, Ray appeared to be merely resting under the dark blankets on his bed. Other convicts on the tier knew what was happening and vigorously supported and encouraged Ray in his endeavor. They did not alert prison officials to the suicide attempt.

On the third day after the cutting, Ray was still not dead. The situation was informally controlled by customs and traditions that had evolved along racial lines. Whites handled their business, blacks theirs, and Hispanics theirs. The white inmate population held Ray accountable to his decision to die. They verbally pressured him to be a real man and not give in to the temptation to call for medical intervention. It was on this third day that Michael passed Ray's cell and looked into Ray's open eyes. Michael saw that Ray wanted help but could not talk.

What Michael did next violated established norms and racial prohibitions. It was a manifestation of the reborn Michael and was based on empathy rather than self-indulgence or the expectation of immediate reward. It did not enhance Michael's reputation among other convicts, black or white. Michael told Ray he would get him medical help unless Ray shook his head to the contrary. Ray's head stayed still, and his penetrating stare was a powerful plea. Against the wishes of other inmates, Michael informed the authorities, who intervened and saved Ray's life.

Ray spent time in the prison hospital and was then returned to the cell block. He and Michael became friends and Michael taught Ray the benefits and mechanics of jogging, weightlifting, and exercise in general. Years later, Ray was paroled. One day, Michael received a postcard. The front of the card was a photograph of Ray finishing the Chicago Marathon. Inscribed on his T-shirt were the names of Ray's team members, including "Iron Mike."

In 1997, Michael was transferred from the penitentiary in Walla Walla to a medium security facility in Airway Heights, near Spokane. He had by then spent nineteen years in prison and was forty-four years old. Washington taxpayers had paid approximately $737,000 to house and feed Michael. They would pay another $1,086,000 over the next twenty-eight years before he was in a position to ask for parole.

Chapter 6

"Patience is not simply the ability to wait—it's how we behave while we're waiting."

—Joyce Meyer

It was Christmas Day 1999, and Michael was feeling sorry for himself. The Airway Heights Correctional Center was less dangerous and intense than the penitentiary, but still grim and very much the picture of modern correctional facilities—lots of razor wire, metal, gravel, clanking doors, protocols, and procedures. Fortunately, the prison had apartments for monthly extended family visits. Michael had just finished his visit with Dee and now faced his twenty-first consecutive Christmas Day alone behind bars. It was another of many holidays separated from his wife and family, but this one felt especially bleak. He was on his knees apologizing and seeking forgiveness—it was the same self-flagellating prayer, the backward-looking prayer he had repeated every day for years. The radio was on and an announcer said something that grabbed Michael's attention and triggered a change in perspective.

"Why are you thinking about all that old stuff? God has something brand new for you. God has given you Isaiah 43:19. Now have yourself a merry little Christmas!"

The song "Have Yourself a Merry Little Christmas" came on and Michael thought he had never heard anything so beautiful. He grabbed his Bible and read and reread the text from Isaiah: "Behold, I am doing a new thing; now it springs forth, do you not perceive it? I will make a way in the wilderness and rivers in the desert."

The language spoke to Michael. It pulled him away from regrets and shame and pointed him forward. It communicated hope and purpose. It was a message that validated the "springing forth" of the transformed Michael whose new life was born of "yatsar"—the Hebrew Old Testament term that describes God's act of forming or fashioning man. Michael called

Dee and shared what he understood to be a powerful message: it was time to dedicate himself to the future.

By the onset of the new millennium Michael had finally and fully accepted himself. He was a sinner, yes, but he was blessed with God's forgiveness, new interpersonal skills, an understanding of his own deep pain, and a conviction that his ongoing life had purpose. His New Year's resolution for 2000 was to focus on ways he could make every encounter with every person a positive experience. He would ensure the resolution applied to everyone—co-workers, friends, acquaintances, strangers, staff, family, clergy. Michael added one important person to the list—himself. He would be mindful of the need to act in a forgiving and compassionate way toward himself.

At the time, he had been working in the prison infirmary as a nurse's aide. It was an opportunity for him to support other inmates in their moment of sickness or death. He bathed them and fed them. He helped many men die and witnessed many of them come to Christ. It was work he believed he was destined to do, work that made him feel whole and integrated. A month into the new year, a job counselor called Michael into her office to ask if he might be interested in working for Omega Pacific Company making mountain climbing equipment at a prison-based work site. The job paid the state's actual minimum wage and was much sought after by other inmates. Ordinarily, you would have to put your name on a long waiting list and even then you could not be guaranteed a job. Michael's name was not on such a list, and it was odd that he would be offered the job without having sought it. He quickly declined the offer because, as he explained to me, "the enemy could be tempting and tricking me into quitting the Lord's work in the infirmary."

The counselor was a pleasant, non-threatening young woman who was perplexed that anyone would turn down this job. She had called Michael in because she thought his corrections record, his work history, and his staff evaluations showed him to be the perfect candidate for the job. It was not judgment but curiosity that caused her to inquire:

"If you don't mind my asking, why would you turn down a job that every other inmate is desperately seeking?"

Michael answered directly. "I think I am meant to minister to the sick and dying. I can make an important contribution in my current job in the infirmary. I am not sure that working for money is a proper way for me to spend my time."

PART 1: RETRIBUTION AND REDEMPTION

The counselor did not intend to talk Michael into accepting the job. She did not want to be antagonistic or defensive. But she did want to make sure Michael was fully cognizant of the proffered job's benefits.

She continued, "I don't doubt your infirmary work is important to you. And I'm sure it's important to the guys you take care of. But it's hard to make more than a pittance in most correctional jobs. This Omega job, on the other hand, would enable you to learn new skills and also send money to your wife. Your work history does not indicate that is something you have ever done. You can contribute to your family and maybe put a little money aside for the future. That may be something you should be thinking about at this stage of your sentence."

The counselor was offering him a chance to make serious money—serious for a convict with a life sentence. It could be the first significant income he earned in decades. She was giving him a chance to be a provider for his family, to plan for the future.

He would pray on it, he told her, and he did. He asked Yahweh through Christ to intervene and stop the process if it was not Yahweh's will for Michael to work for money. He reasoned that prison authorities had picked him for a new job. He was bound to abide by their will absent some contrary sign from God. No such sign appeared, and in February of 2000 Michael went to work for the private employer. He worked for Omega until 2004 and made over $40,000. He was by then a fifty-year-old man who, for the first time in his life, was proud of the way he provided for his family. The employment situation also gave him a chance to work on his goal of making each encounter a positive experience. He formed new friendships and explored new ways to support co-workers and supervisors.

When the parole board met in 2004, it was impressed with Michael's progress. He was now fifty-one years old and had spent the last decade learning how to live with inmates, staff, and himself. His employment history was exemplary, he had good reviews from prison counselors, and was considered to be a model prisoner. His faith, his family, and his commitment to therapy and self-healing were all contributing factors. Still, he was serving consecutive life sentences and the board was obliged to remind him that he would have to serve some proportional amount of time on each sentence before he could be considered "rehabilitated." The board rewarded Michael's progress by ending his parole on several Benton County convictions and transitioning him to begin his sentences on the Franklin County convictions entered by Judge Knight. After twenty-six years in prison, Michael was still facing multiple life terms in prison, but fewer than before.

Michael resumed his job as a nurse's aide when his employment with Omega ended in 2004, as a result of the state's termination of paid private employment for prisoners. He spent the next eight years at the Airway Heights Correctional Center. These were calm and trouble-free years. He avoided turbulence and discord among inmates and, when possible, actively intervened to mediate and prevent potentially violent confrontations. He grew in confidence and self-esteem. The prison community knew him to be dependable, compassionate, and nonviolent. Michael's life had meaning, and he enjoyed living it.

His wife continued to see him for extended family visits. Her mother, Pearletha, was central to both their lives, especially after Michael turned to Jesus in 1990. He loved his mother-in-law and was deeply saddened when she died in 2004. Fortunately, he was able to say goodbye. Pearletha had visited Michael at the Airway Heights prison shortly before returning to her home in Chicago and being hospitalized. Michael remembers her smile and shining eyes as she turned to say goodbye at the end of her visit. It was a final, spiritual goodbye, and left a permanent imprint. He also remembers their last telephone conversation just moments before she took her last breath. He said, "I love you, Pearletha. Please tell Jesus 'hello' and thank him for all he has done for me." Dee was in the hospital room with her mother and held the phone. Pearletha whispered, "I will" and died while Michael prayed for her soul in his prison cell 1,800 miles away.

Michael remained committed to his faith and became deeply involved with the prison ministry. His age and wisdom were put to use in quelling clashes and potential violence among younger inmates. He modeled non-violence even when he was the target of violent attacks. When provoked, he retreated, and found ways to defuse the situation. He pursued opportunities to speak with other inmates who were receptive to learning how to change their behavior and their lives.

Michael's mother stayed in regular touch from Chicago by telephone and letters. When she could afford it, she would visit Michael at the prison and stay with Dee in Pasco. Michael's children also kept in touch. They were grown and the younger two were now married with their own children. Michael was moving into late middle age. His life was as good as he might expect in a controlled environment.

PART 1: RETRIBUTION AND REDEMPTION

There were, however, new and different challenges. On March 18, 2011, Michael was taken to a Spokane hospital for testing as a result of urinary issues. On the way back to the prison, chained in the back of a police car, he was given the news that he had prostate cancer. He immediately interpreted the news as a spiritual challenge. He said to himself, "Now we are going to see what you are really made of." This was just one more way the adversary would attempt to wreak havoc. Michael believed in the power of prayer and the power of living his life according to Yahweh's will. He presented his circumstances to the Lord and faced surgery with confidence. The surgery—a complete prostatectomy—was successful and Michael has been cancer free ever since.

* * * *

In 2012, Michael was transferred to the Coyote Ridge Correctional Center in Connell. The transfer was requested and granted because the Coyote Ridge facility was closer to Pasco and had finally established an extended family visitation program that would allow Dee to see and spend time with Michael without the inconvenience and expense involved in traveling to Airway Heights. He was put to work as lead custodian in the correctional industry food factory, where he managed a staff of three and was responsible for maintenance and cleanliness of factory workspace and offices. When he was not working, he studied, prayed, exercised, and participated in prison personal development programs. He received certificates for completing several courses: "Right Living," "Getting it Right," "Making it Work," and "Anger and Stress Management." As had been true at the Airway Heights prison, Michael read books but did not watch television. He had turned a life of chaos, hedonism, and hurt into uninterrupted days, months, and years of discipline, usefulness, and personal growth.

In 2015, he was suffering the ill effects of Hepatitis C, which he had contracted while using needles to shoot heroin during his early years at the penitentiary in the 1980s. Correctional policy at the time prevented inmates over sixty years of age from receiving treatment at the state's expense. Michael was sixty-two and was told he would not be treated. He prayed. A month later, he was called in for a medical consultation and advised that the administrators at the central correctional office in Olympia, the state capital, had directed the prison to begin a work-up to determine if he would benefit from a revolutionary new Hepatitis C cure consisting of taking Harvoni oral tablets. Michael started the treatment on May 6, 2015. He took a pill a day for several weeks. Each tablet sold for $1,200. In the end, the treatment cost the state of Washington close to $100,000. Michael was cured of Hepatitis C. He credits the Lord and increasingly progressive Department of Corrections medical policies.

He has prevailed over lesser medical challenges as well. Today, he is in excellent health and requires no medication of any kind. Michael does not take this for granted. He is grateful for the quality of his medical care but also recognizes that his good health and good fortune are attributable to his commitment to walk a different path after 1990.

During the twenty-two years since Michael left the state penitentiary, there was only one disciplinary incident that was sufficiently noteworthy to be entered into Michael's disciplinary record. In 2006, he asked the nondenominational prison chaplain at Airway Heights for permission to be baptized by Michael's Protestant minister from Spokane. The chaplain approved the requested ceremony but would not approve anyone but himself as the officiant of a Protestant baptism. Michael requested a face-to-face meeting at which he calmly but insistently argued that he should have the right to pick his own minister and that, as far as he knew, there was no institutional or Department of Corrections regulation that prevented it. At some point, the chaplain told Michael the decision had been made and the discussion was over. Michael kept talking and was written up for an infraction: "failure to disperse when asked." This was the first and only record of a disciplinary lapse in Michael's prison record between 1991 and 2019.

Chapter 7

"The last place I would ever want to go is prison."

—Martha Stewart

I listened to "The Long and Winding Road" and "Here Comes the Sun" as I drove south from Spokane on a broad highway that ran straight and flat through the eastern Washington desert. When you drive the same road year after year, lost in thought, listening to the Beatles, and the landscape is unchanging—the sagebrush, the road signs, the distant hills—it is possible to forget exactly where you are in the chronology of your life. It could have been 1977 or 1997. It was, in fact, October 2017 and I was white-haired, a retired old law professor absorbed in the enduring melodies and lyrics of my expectant youth.

I was headed for the Coyote Ridge Correctional Center to visit Michael. He had a timeless quality too, like the Beatles, but his came from being banished, unseen, and ghostly, an icon who represents the darkness we wish to keep at bay. He had achieved the timelessness that comes from being a lifer. I drove, distracted and pensive, poking around in dormant memories, possessed by the gloom that seemed always to attend my visits to a state prison. Listening to John Lennon's plaintive voice did not help. It evoked sad thoughts of his death in 1980 and steered me back to the fact that Michael had already been locked up for almost three years when Lennon died. I switched to an iPhone collection featuring Marvin Gaye. "Don't punish me with brutality/Come on talk to me/So you can see/What's going on." It seemed more fitting. I knew I would feel hollow and small when I entered the prison. Correctional officers would lock the doors behind me, and there would be friction when I rubbed against their authority. I would be in the presence of sad men whose suffering might last to the end of their days.

Connell has a forlorn, almost eerie feel. It might be just another dusty and forgettable small town, a place to stop for gas or coffee before moving on. But the Coyote Ridge prison inhabits the quiet community like a collection of dead souls haunts a cemetery. I exited the freeway and found a Circle K convenience store on Connell's main street near the center of town. A few pickup trucks were parked out front, belonging to farmers and cowboys, I supposed. An attractive young Hispanic woman leaned over the cash register chatting quietly in Spanish with another young woman who did not appear to be a customer. I waited and felt conspicuous in my coat and tie, wondering why, after all these years, I still needed to dress like a lawyer. The cashier glanced at me, straightened, and forced a smile. Her confidant, alerted to my presence, politely moved aside so I could pay for my coffee.

"Hi, ladies. How is life in beautiful downtown Connell this morning?" I inquired. It was a snarky question, but one that acknowledged the common understanding that, whatever might be said about Connell, it did not have a beautiful downtown.

The cashier was forgiving. "Oh, it could be worse. We could be in prison." She grinned.

"Come on, the prison's not so bad," the other woman said. "I know lots of people who work there. Of course, they get to leave after work."

"Well, that's where I'm headed," I offered, as though my destination was some big mystery.

"Keep your head down, dude, and your butt to the wall," the cashier kidded. She gave me change and returned to gossiping with her companion.

I carried the steaming cup to my car and sat, engine off, uneasy and inert. The rich Kona aroma enveloped me, and I inhaled deeply, closed my eyes, found and focused on a cosmically green color in the middle of my mind, a color that substituted for a mantra when I didn't have time for a proper meditation. I was preparing for Michael and the unfathomable truth that he had spent the last forty years in prison. My short coffee break and meditation morphed into an unruly rumination.

A part of me was weightless, floating, the untethered imagination of a retiree who could now forsake his former world, or the world in general, maybe travel, or search for God, or improve his slice-prone golf game, or sit at the seashore with a pile of books and a big, bouncing labradoodle. Another part of me was heavy and weary, beleaguered with memories, of things done and left undone, the residue of the past. There it was—my life compressed but expansive—all that time, all that had happened, all that it meant, and, yet, how brief and dreamlike and vaporous. I sipped coffee in a Circle K parking lot, in this lonely little town, overwhelmed by memories pruned and distorted by time. I finally focused on a few fragments I knew to be true: the fading image of a young lawyer who believed the arc of history really did bend towards justice; and the image of another young man, a black man in chains, a lost soul condemned to die behind bars.

I was procrastinating, but it was okay. I had arrived in Connell well in advance of my scheduled meeting so that I could approach the lockup in unhurried steps. I had a powerful desire to escape feelings of discomfort. More than anything, I wanted to diminish and reconcile the emotional dissonance one might feel at a zoo—the jarring sense of anomaly and impropriety in watching, for example, the unnatural circumstances of a great African elephant confined forever to a few square feet in a concrete cage. Michael Anderson, of course, was not an African elephant. He was merely an old man, a kindly husband and father who, in his youth, had been in great pain and had caused great pain.

Five minutes to 10:00. I started the car, eased onto Main Street, and drove slowly north. A city cop followed me to the city limits. The road narrowed to a winding, one-way lane carved from sagebrush and sunbaked dirt that stretched across a broad and treeless valley floor to a distant mesa. About a half mile farther, the road ended at a complex of stark rectangular buildings surrounded by asphalt, gravel, and razor-wire fences. The design was modern but unmistakably derivative of society's long history of warehousing lawbreakers in uninviting settings far from their loved ones. The images transported me back to that time, decades ago, when I first visited Michael at another prison, the Washington State Penitentiary. I have never forgotten the heaviness of the place, the cold, inhospitable look and feel of penal duress. The sensations return whenever I visit prisons, drive by prisons, hear about prisons, or contemplate the fact that the United States imprisons more people, and at a higher rate, than any other country in the world.

I parked in the designated lot at the Coyote Ridge prison, sat for a moment, and braced myself against the vague apprehension that I, too, was somehow unworthy; that my flawed existence would be discovered, excavated, and deconstructed; that all I really needed for self-improvement was to be in a controlled environment that eliminated personal autonomy and bad decisions. The feeling was reinforced when an intimidating German Shepard circled and sniffed me immediately after I entered the door marked for visitors. I announced my name and purpose to the security official at the desk, giving him both my driver's license and bar association card. He checked to see if I had received the necessary advance clearance from prison administrators. There was a bank of lockers on the left and

I was instructed to lock up everything except my clothes and briefcase. I then took off my shoes and belt, placed them in a basket, gave the official my briefcase, and walked through the x-ray machine three times, each time triggering its alarm. The guard then probed my whole body with his hands, including my crotch area, and finally concluded the metal buttons on my slacks had set off the alarm. My briefcase apparently passed muster even though it contained, in addition to legal papers, a copy of my recently published book that I had brought as a gift for Michael.

After clearing security, I was introduced to Anderson's counselor, Joseph, and we proceeded through two metal gates electronically controlled by a guard who sat in a secure control room peering out a thick plexiglass window. The last gate opened to the outdoors and a series of concentric razor-wire fences, each about twelve feet in height and separated by roughly fifty feet of gravel. The walk across this open space between guard houses and barbed wire reinforced the inescapable and unalterable fact of a prisoner's confinement. The counselor and I finally arrived at an interior building that contained a large visiting room with vending machines and a central guard station. As we waited for the heavy door to slide open, I chatted with Joseph.

"How long have you known Anderson?"

"Not long, he was assigned to me a couple of months ago."

"So, is he a good guy, a good inmate?" I tried to be casual.

"I've had no problems with him. He's respectful, does not make trouble, does his work, and helps the young inmates." He paused, then, "He's been in the system a long time."

"Yes, I know. Too long." The counselor sensed that I was trying to get his opinion on the matter.

"Can't say too much on that, not my call."

Joseph and a guard took me into the small room off to the side that was designated for inmate meetings with lawyers. There was a table and a couple of chairs. I was told to wait. Joseph said he had things to attend to and excused himself. The room was institutional and lifeless—all metal and plastic with a surveillance camera in an upper corner and a large plexiglass window that opened onto a walkway regularly traversed by prison guards. There was nothing soft, nothing warm, no color, no art, and no incentive to stay any longer than necessary. I was starting to shrink, like a snail that feels threatened. The walls were not friendly barriers that protected me from external danger. They *were* the danger, and they seemed to get closer and closer. I retreated into my thoughts, and waited, now anxious to see and talk to Michael after an interruption of several years in our curious, unfolding relationship.

Time had washed over our lives since I represented Michael in the late 1970s. Days, years, decades rolled by, sometimes in a trickle of mindless repetition, other times as a flood that changed everything, all of it eroding the sharp edges of our youth and reshaping our lives. I had become a law school professor, law school dean, world traveler, husband, father, and graybeard with a declining golf game. I was accustomed to professional and vacation travel to Hawaii, Europe, the Middle East, South America, and Asia. In my world, surrounded by people who shared my background, these activities were not exceptional.

Michael Anderson, on the other hand, had spent almost 15,000 days in a five-by-ten-foot cell. He also was surrounded by people who shared his background—fatherless, traumatized, poorly educated, and lost. He and his wife had a third child, now well into his thirties, conceived after Michael went to the penitentiary. They had become grandparents and great grandparents many times over. The court's hope that Michael should die in prison was getting ever closer to fulfillment. Yes, Michael might well linger here until his death, in this dispiriting place where I was now sitting, even though he was a model prisoner, and even though his last major violation of any prison rule—the most notable standard by which rehabilitation is measured—was recorded in 1991, some twenty-seven years before.

A guard interrupted my reverie. He ushered Michael into the visiting room, and I rose to meet a handsome, relaxed, and smiling black man with short gray hair dressed in pressed khaki prison garb. Michael looked me in the eye and grabbed me. Our hug was heartfelt and true, an embrace of body and spirit that connected us to all that we had been and all that we had become.

"It's been a long time, George. It's good to see you."

"It's good to see you too, Michael. You look well." I meant it. Michael was glowing. "How you doing?"

"I'm fine. Every day's a blessing," he said, succinctly separating himself from the attitude of most inmates. "I knew you would come."

I grinned. "How could you be so sure? I don't spend much time in out-of-the-way prisons anymore."

"Ah, you were always there for me, George. But the reason I was sure you'd come is because it's the Lord's will."

I knew that faith had been a central part of Michael's life for many years, but I did not want to think of myself as a player in some divine drama.

"Well, I don't know about the Lord, Mike, but it really is nice to see you and I'm happy to help you in any way I can."

Michael was not deterred by my spiritual diffidence. He smiled. There was nothing smug in his demeanor, no sense of entitlement in his delivery. His confidence had been earned the hard way.

"There's a plan for me, and you're part of it. The first step is to get me out of here. It's time for me to be paroled."

We chatted, shared information about one another's families, and spoke of possible strategies for presenting Michael's case at his next parole hearing. The conversation was easy, and our limited time together was too soon at an end. I could not help but be awed by Michael's calm and clear way of being. He spoke without shame or guile, displayed no trace of recrimination, and harbored no ill will. His surroundings had not materially changed in forty years, but he appeared to have evolved to the point of walking among the enlightened ones. Whatever the case, this was not the man I first met in 1979, the wounded man from Illinois who brought crime and hurt to eastern Washington.

Before leaving, I handed Michael the copy of the paperback I brought for him as a gift. He looked at the book, thanked me heartily, but quickly returned it to me, explaining that he could not directly receive any written material from a visitor. All such material had to go through authorized channels and be screened in accordance with Department of Corrections policy. He advised me to mail the book to him, and it would hopefully get to him after the screening process. Michael was institutionalized, but I was not.

"That's ridiculous, the book is here now," I declared. "I'll just give it to one of the guards and request that it be approved for delivery to you."

I got up and approached the door to speak with a guard standing outside our meeting room. Michael shook his head, indicating that was not the proper protocol. I waved him off.

"Don't worry," I said. "I'm sure they'll accept a book from me. Not only am I your lawyer, I wrote the damn book."

The guard looked at the book, returned it to me and said I would have to mail it, and it would need to go through the customary process. I said I understood that, but couldn't the guard just take the book and transfer it to whoever had responsibility for screening written materials?

No, that was inconsistent with prison procedure. I put the book back into my briefcase and forgot about it.

The next day I received an email from the Assistant Superintendent of the Coyote Ridge Correctional Center informing me that my visitation privileges at the prison had been terminated due to my attempt to "smuggle contraband, i.e. unapproved written materials, into the prison."

Chapter 8

"And no wonder, for even Satan disguises himself as an Angel of Light."

—2 Corinthians 11:14

The governor appoints Washington's parole board members, and they have wide latitude in deciding how much time Michael Anderson should serve on each of his ten consecutive life sentences. The board establishes a minimum term for each sentence, and, when that term is completed, the board might add additional time to the sentence, depending on the offender's behavior and progress, or allow the clock to start ticking on the minimum term for the next consecutive life sentence. By 2017, Anderson had endured multiple parole hearings. I had not seen him for a long time, but every time I thought of him, I sensed the weariness of Morgan Freeman's character in the movie *Shawshank Redemption* when he faced repeated and pitiless denials of parole.

As it happened, Michael had contacted me just after I retired from my job as a tenured professor at Gonzaga University School of Law—the exact time I was looking for a way to make good use of my skills as a lawyer without getting entangled in enervating legal warfare. I was more than happy to walk with Michael on this last stretch of the journey we had started together so many years ago. I felt that in addition to my opportunity to help him, he had something to teach me. My sense was that this "something" was not the gospel, *per se*, and it was not about pious living. It had something to do with awakening in me a sensibility about integration and synthesis that had laid dormant for many years. Michael touched my yearning to stop compartmentalizing and to reconnect my many disparate parts.

When I visited Michael at the Coyote Ridge Correctional Center in the fall of 2017, he had been a model prisoner for decades. His prison work record in both the food, health care, and private employment sectors was stellar. He had become known as a mentor of young inmates who needed guidance about how to adapt positively to the rigors and danger of prison life. He was also known for his efforts to defuse potential violence among inmates who were at odds. The prison ministry depended on his participation and enthusiasm. Dee continued to see him every month for extended family visits that enabled the couple to maintain and deepen their marital commitment, their shared faith, and their effort to address concerns and challenges affecting their family. Dee also visited on other occasions when she could bring one or more of their extended family. Michael and Dee now had sixteen grandchildren and five great-grandchildren. They had all visited Michael at one time or another, and he felt blessed every time any of his far-flung offspring visited from distant cities.

Michael was well into his sixties. His life in prison was routine. His relationships with staff and inmates were conflict-free. His mind was calm, his spirit bright and buoyant, and he was free of the destructive passions and impulses that had ruled his early years.

After forty years of confinement, he was institutionalized, and he knew it. He had never held a cell phone, never run a Google search, and could not recall what it was like to experience silence. The institution decided what he would eat and when. The fragrance of freshly bloomed flowers could be imagined, but, like so many simple pleasures, it was nothing more than a decades-old memory. The sounds of his world were sharp and metallic. There was wind in a dusty prison yard, but no wind against the trees, no trees at all, and no quiet moments under the stars. Michael's fear that he would spend his life needing to ask permission to use the bathroom had come true.

What might it be like to reenter the world? What would it be like to be surrounded by loved ones, to give back to the wife who had stood beside him and deserved so much, to be with his family and part of a community in ways that honored all that he learned, his faith in God, and his abiding belief that, while he could not change the past, he could help light the way for young people who lived in darkness?

Close your eyes and imagine, just imagine, the feel of walking barefoot down a sandy beach, a happy, playful dog at your side, ocean waves rising and falling, the sun on the western horizon, still warm, and you have all evening to stroll, if you like, and breathe the sea air, and choose freely to walk until the moon lights the night sky, and then, when you're ready, return to your family, your grandchildren and great grandchildren, all of them singing songs you've never heard, just beyond the dunes, around a big bonfire that shoots sparks high into the air. And you pause and marvel at it all—the children, the sand and sea and sky, and the rising sparks, twinkling and luminous, sparks that soon die out but not before they brighten the darkness and mingle with a trillion stars.

Michael's earliest possible release date established by the parole board in the 1980s was 2059, when he would be 106 years old. This was adjusted to 2025 in 1996. In 2011, the parole board decided to end his minimum sentence on all but three of his consecutive life sentences. This meant that in another five years or so, it would be feasible and potentially realistic for Michael to ask for acceleration of the date of his actual parole on the last of his consecutive sentences. My job would be to help Michael convince the parole board to advance his release date from 2025 to around 2021 or earlier. He hoped to spend his seventies with Dee and his extended family, giving support and guidance to his grandchildren and their children, and ministering to young men at risk of spending their lives the way he spent his. His parole hearing was scheduled for March 20, 2018, the vernal equinox, the time when light balances the dark, a time of emotional symmetry and new beginnings. The date had great significance for Michael for it validated and bore witness to his truth and his experience. There were things he did not know, but he surely understood the interplay between light and darkness.

* * * *

Judges had long ago urged that Michael never be released from prison. How could Michael and I convince the parole board that now was the time, indeed—past time, to finally recognize that a young out-of-control, violent predator had evolved into a loving, faith-based, sixty-five-year-old great-grandfather who would dedicate his freedom to good works? I knew society and the board might harbor some vague suspicion that Michael's rehabilitation was a mere pretense and deception, the manipulation of a disturbed con man who has patiently and cleverly used religion and psychological jargon to construct a façade of normality while still fantasizing about domination, intimidation, the infliction of pain, control and revenge.

I had recently read *The Adversary: A True Story of Monstrous Deception*, a book by the French author Emmanuel Carrère. It tells the bizarre and horrific tale of a father who murdered his wife, children, and parents when they discovered he was a con man and an impostor. The accused was diagnosed as having a narcissistic personality so pronounced, smooth, and nuanced that for eighteen years he was able to persuade friends, family, and strangers that he was both a medical doctor (he wasn't) and an investment broker with access to special accounts that promised high rates of return (in fact, he stole investors' funds). Because these acts of deception were so skillful and pervasive, psychologists speculated that it was possible the murderer had come to believe his false persona was real. Shortly after being sentenced to twenty-five years in prison, the murderer claimed he turned to God and religion and was now living in the light surrounded by love. The book's author digs down on this claim of spiritual transformation and finds evidence of dishonesty, manipulation, and grandiose thinking on the murderer's part that continued for years after he had entered prison. The author ends his book with the following questions:

> He is not putting on an act, of that I am sure, but isn't the liar inside him putting one over on him? When Christ enters his heart, when the certainty of being loved in spite of everything makes tears of joy run down his cheeks, isn't it the adversary deceiving him yet again?

The author was uncertain about the answers.

As Michael Anderson's lawyer, it was not necessary for me personally to be convinced of his conversion. My professional responsibility was to act as his voice and his advocate. I would marshal facts and information, identify the legal rules, and try to make an effective argument in favor of his release from prison.

But I did not want to invest the time and labor in writing this book unless I could sincerely vouch for Michael's character, his religious authenticity, and his potential for making a positive contribution to the world beyond prison walls. Why? Because Michael hoped the book would be a platform for reaching out to people who believed not only in the possibility of rehabilitation, but in salvation and grace through Christ. I did not wish to become a player in a dangerous and complicated drama directed by an "adversary" who might still have power over Michael's mental health, much less an "adversary" who threatened Michael's soul and lusted after my own. If I was going to play a role in telling Michael Anderson's story and promoting the lesson of his life to true believers and spiritual seekers, I needed to be sure he was the genuine article.

My heart told me Michael was, in fact, the real deal. We had a relationship of mutual recognition and regard that bridged decades and the great chasm separating our lived experiences. I also had objective proof of Michael's authenticity. The proof was in Michael's good works, not just his profession of faith. It was in his constancy and continual growth over three decades. It was his family's enduring commitment and loyalty under circumstances that would have tested the most forgiving and ardent among us. It is revealed in the lives of prisoners he has helped and in his positive relationship with people in authority.

Michael and I did not share identical views about life and the transcendent, but I looked forward to telling his story—both to the parole board and the larger world.

Part 2: Darkness

Chapter 9

"I knew I needed something, but I didn't know what..."
—Michael Anderson

Abigail loved him but in an incomplete way. No one had ever said "I love you" to her and she never uttered those words to baby Michael. Years later, when he learned that his mother was emotionally wounded, he began to understand why she had never held his hand, stroked him, hugged him, kissed him, or curled up with him to read a children's book. It was the same with his stepfather, Andy, a big man, a Korean War veteran who worked as a security guard. Andy's own father had been murdered when Andy was a young boy and he was raised by a single mother with no male role model. Like Abigail, Andy was never able to say, "I love you." He could not look Michael in the eye, could not ask him "What's wrong, son?" and could not, did not, show affection. Michael's biological dad was not in the picture—he had abandoned Michael at birth.

Michael was born in 1953 on June 3. He and his mother lived in the basement of her mother's house, a three-level flat at the corner of 43rd and Evans on Chicago's south side, an area of the city known as the Black Belt, the name assigned after white wealth fled to the suburbs and discriminatory real estate practices limited where African Americans could live.

Baby Michael was a sensitive child, and physically beautiful. According to Abigail, he was "the sweetest child you could want." People would say he should have been born a girl, he was so cute. Michael recalls feeling hollow as a child, but Abigail remembered that he could be adorable and good-hearted and that he remained so, at least toward her, even after his destructive impulses came to dominate his life. He would occasionally get up early, cook eggs and bacon, and bring her breakfast in bed. The bacon was never quite cooked but the affection he showed was touching. When Michael was five years old, she bought him a bicycle. Shortly thereafter, Michael happened to speak with the garbage man who complimented him on his new bike. The man mentioned that he hoped someday to be able to buy a bicycle for his own son. Michael gave his bike to the garbage man on the spot. When Abigail asked him where his bike had gone, Michael told her he felt sorry for the garbage man's son.

In time, another little Michael emerged, a Michael drawn to violence. He was six years old when he and children from the neighborhood decided to explore the musty back room of his grandmother's garage, a place littered with boxes, mattresses, and old car parts. They discovered the rusting frame of a 1928 Model A Ford. The vehicle's back seat was a remnant skeleton consisting of tattered upholstery and visible springs that long ago may have cushioned the ride of some proud owner. A foot-long piece of fabric survived in the very middle of the old seat. On it was a mother cat with a new litter of baby kittens. Michael looked into the disintegrating wreck, saw the litter, and calmly picked up a brick that he flung onto the heap of fragile felines. The neighbor children watched in horror and ran from the garage to report Michael's cruelty to his mother. Michael remembers the incident but does not associate it with any feeling. He can only speculate that somehow he experienced a covetous and wrathful response to the image of babies nestled around the warmth of a nurturing mother.

He had a "big brother," Martez, who was not really a brother but a cousin. Michael and Martez became close when Andy moved the family in with Martez's family, just down the street from Michael's grandmother's house. Michael idolized Martez even after the older boy was shot and paralyzed while participating in a robbery. Martez, barely an adolescent, died from his injuries soon after, leaving young Michael fractured by the violence and the loss. But the family did not talk about such things. Andy had survived combat in Korea and trauma in his own family history. These experiences created in him a belief that the best way to manage emotional discomfort was to ignore it and move on. Michael had no language for sharing his grief, and no model, no opportunity, no sympathetic ear for talking about feelings of sadness. He learned to hide his emotions. They were eventually buried, and Michael gradually started to become numb.

Andy moved the family again, this time to a rental property at 45th and Ellis, a property that prohibited children. Michael and his younger brother and sister circumvented the restriction by sneaking in and out of the house through the back door. There was no way the children could fully grasp the implications of an arrangement that required deception and pretense aimed at concealing where they lived. Michael remembers being embarrassed but can only guess at how it may have contributed to a growing sense that he did not fit in or, worse, was unwanted.

A stepsister was born in 1960. In 1962, Andy moved the growing family again, this time to the projects located at 109th and Racine. They had a brick house with three bedrooms and a basement. Michael was enrolled in elementary school but was not interested. He lacked discipline and sought attention by being disruptive. His focus turned more and more to the streets. And bicycles. By the time Michael was ten years old, his favorite pastime was stealing bicycles. He would soon graduate to stealing cars. Abigail consulted a school psychologist who said Michael was a natural leader who needed structure and responsibilities. It was too late. Michael was already seriously damaged. He dropped out of school for good in 1965, when he was twelve, about the time his stepbrother, Robert, was born. Abigail now had five young children and it was easy for Michael to disappear.

Years later, Michael came to understand that this period of his early adolescence—he calls it the "Racine Courts" period—was psychologically and spiritually pivotal. "Something extraordinary happened to me in the Racine Courts," Michael said in 2019, "something unnatural, something unclean." A nightmare, always the same, consumed him night after night. He would go to sleep in fear that a menacing force would enter the house. In the dream, he repeatedly tried to lock the back door without success. A demon would find the door ajar, enter, and take refuge in the basement where he called out to Michael to join him in the darkness. Michael would struggle, would try to resist, but did not know how to defend himself. The nightmare left him feeling scared but strangely connected to the powerful force that dwelled below. Years later he would become a real-life terror who concealed himself in a basement, in Pasco, Washington, while the family slept upstairs.

After dropping out of school, Michael roamed the inner-city streets when he was not in juvenile detention or jail. His friends were like him—constantly looking for something that made them feel good. There was freedom in the streets, but it was a negative freedom that mainly provided periodic respite from unhappiness and vulnerability. It was freedom to steal, to use drugs, to impose one's will, to be in control, and to search for comfort. Michael's world gradually narrowed to activities that served one purpose only—the avoidance of pain. Year by year, crime by crime, he became a kind of vampire. He lived in the shadows seeking excitement and gratification that, paradoxically, would render him insensible.

Michael and the demon of his dreams began to blend. The darkness got blacker and deeper. He could not know what he knows today—that every theft or lie or assault made the next hurtful act easier. Every step down made him want to take another step because he felt more powerful and he believed that power was his to use and control. He could not comprehend that, in fact, he had no power. He could not say no, could not delay gratification, could not see beyond himself, his immediate needs, and the moment. There was a part of him that wished he "could be a better person" but there was no visible bridge for getting there, and no real sense of the rewards that might flow from being a better person, even if he could get there.

The one positive activity that counteracted the darkness during his first decade of life was his brief participation in a neighborhood Cub Scouts troop. Each troop member was tasked with performing "good deeds" as part of the Cub Scouts' ethos and mission. Michael felt happy and safe with the Cub Scouts and looked forward to scouting events and friendships. But his stepfather terminated his Cub Scouts affiliation as punishment for starting a house fire when the ten-year-old boy accidentally lit glue on fire while trying to fix a punctured bicycle tire. Later, his former scouting friends periodically told him how much fun they had on camping trips and other scouting activities.

When he was eleven years old, Michael was sent to Audy Home, a juvenile detention center located on Roosevelt Road. He was there for truancy, stealing, and running away from home. It was his first experience with incarceration. Audy Home was established in 1899 as one the first juvenile detention centers in the country. It was intended to separate juveniles from adult detainees and to provide a humane model of education and punishment. In fact, the center was chronically underfunded and failed to achieve its progressive goals. Juvenile inmates were beaten by grown men—brutal and unapologetic guards whose correctional strategy was the imposition of pain and punishment for the most innocuous rules violation. Michael remembers the Christmas when the children were required to line up for distribution of holiday gifts. A drunk guard hurled the gifts at each recipient as his name was called. A package smashed into one young boy's face, breaking his nose in an explosion of blood.

Michael returned from the Audy Home to a mother who felt affection for her son but could not guide or protect him. She had her own emotional shortcomings and was busy with her other young children and a domineering husband. To make matters worse, Andy had developed a fondness for alcohol, which often induced him to try to break Michael by whipping him with straps and extension cords. Abigail recalled that, at this point, Michael was completely out of control and that "whippings never seemed to help him." Andy had limited parenting skills and little understanding of Michael's emotional needs or the fact that his behavior was shaped by the absence of intimate support infants normally get from their mothers. The family dynamics were also complicated by Andy's understandable but misguided insistence that Michael submit to him as though he was his real father. In the stubborn and rebellious chaos that dictated Michael's dysfunction, that was never going to happen. He refused to surrender to Andy, and this escalated their discord.

Michael has many memories about Andy, but one story lies irrepressibly and poignantly at his psychic core. Andy once asked Michael to retrieve Andy's wristwatch from the car. Michael did so, and he ran back to his stepfather expecting praise for the effort. Instead, Andy admonished Michael: "Why were you running? Don't you know you could have broken the watch? That watch means more to me than you do!"

Andy could impose a range of punishments. Once, fourteen-year-old Michael took Andy's 1967 Pontiac Bonneville for a joyride in the middle of the night. When the neighbors reported to Andy that they had seen Michael driving the car, Andy was unable to control his rage. He delivered a blow to the side of Michael's head with a 357 Magnum pistol, an assault that turned out to be a precursor to Michael's own criminal conduct over a decade later when he pistol-whipped an innocent mother and housewife who inadvertently discovered him hiding in her Pasco, Washington basement.

The blow to Michael's head did not end Andy's punishment. He handcuffed Michael to his bed, saying that he had no option since Michael could not be trusted. For several days Michael slept with one wrist handcuffed to the metal bedframe, his shame profound, his rage ascendant. The cuffs were finally removed after Michael's brother informed their mother that Michael had defecated on the bedroom floor. Many years later, Abigail remembered this episode and, during a prison visit, apologized to Michael.

This story of a broken relationship between a boy and his stepfather runs deeper, though, and there is a dimension to it that makes it heartbreakingly lamentable. In his own rough and rudimentary way, Andy tried to be a father. He talked to the boy about how to survive in white society, how to manage interaction with people in authority, and about the kind of employment possibilities Michael should be thinking about. He took Michael hunting and fishing a few times and sometimes let him ride along on day trips to destinations in and beyond the city. Andy's beatings, too, must be seen in context. While sometimes delivered in anger and frustration, they were prompted by the goal of keeping Michael out of trouble. Harsh physical discipline was perhaps not so uncommon in working-class families of the time, and Andy presumably had no understanding of the mental health risks associated with corporal punishment.

Over time, Andy demonstrated genuine interest in Michael by visiting him in the various Illinois jail and prison settings where Michael was destined to be incarcerated. In 1974, just before Andy and Abigail divorced, Andy visited Michael at the Illinois State Penitentiary in Joliet where Michael was doing time for attempted murder and robbery. Both parties faked it. The younger man played the role of the regretful son who had disappointed the nurturing father. The older man pretended they had had storybook lives that inexplicably went wrong. As they parted, the dynamic changed, and the stubborn truth of their painful, conjoined lives rose up and produced tears that embarrassed them both. They had never shared feelings, except for anger, but each man knew the other man felt hollow and unhappy. Now they struggled awkwardly to find a way to acknowledge their shared pain and affirm that each had meant something to the other. The stepfather and stepson said goodbye and put their palms together on the opposite sides of the glass window that separated them. It was the last time they saw one another.

* * * *

What is clear in retrospect is that Michael could have used a loving father, biological or otherwise. Sitting in his prison cell in 2019, gray and a bit shrunken, Michael wrote:

"I made so many people's lives worse because they had an encounter with me. I wreaked havoc and did not understand that my conduct would cause me to pay a great debt. I did not know there would be a reaping and a sowing. I needed a father. A father gives his children instruction, protection, sustenance, companionship, assistance, love, and discipline. A father is an example for his children."

PART 2: DARKNESS

He had a biological father, of course, but the man never visited Michael and never supported him. Michael initially got his father's name but even that was taken from him when Andy adopted Michael and legally changed his name. He was not supposed to talk about his father, or see him, because the father was said to be no good. Instead, the only significant adult male in Michael's life was the stepfather who beat him and demanded that Michael address him as "Dad."

Yet Michael always thought about his real dad and harbored thoughts of a possible meeting. To act on this desire, however, would invite his mother's displeasure. He knew his biological father had an automobile repair shop at the corner of 43rd and Evans in south Chicago, not far from Michael's home. While still a young boy in grade school, before Andy came on the scene, he would sometimes walk to the shop and observe his dad from a distance. He would position himself behind the fenders of parked cars and intently watch his father's every move. There was something he needed, but he didn't know what.

One day, his real father saw him peering from behind parked cars. He recognized him, bought him an ice cream cone, and gave him a silver dollar. This was the only time in Michael's life that he had verbal contact with his father. When Michael got home, he told his mother and grandmother he found the silver dollar. They believed him. The whole experience left him confused and frustrated. But he learned one valuable lesson that eventually contributed to his way of being as an adolescent and young adult. He learned that people believed him when he lied.

There is a chance, a slim chance at best, that Michael's path could have been different. His maternal grandfather is remembered as a positive and loving presence in Michael's infancy. Michael's memory about this is both visceral and graphic. There is a warm, smiling face teaching baby Michael how to walk. The grandfather's arms are extended, his words filled with encouragement and praise. There is touching and more—hugs, even kisses. Michael was still very young when they took his grandfather away in an ambulance. He never saw him again.

Curiously, Abigail stated in 2019, at age eighty-nine, that she did not believe Michael could have conscious memories of his grandfather, because he was so young when her father died. She wondered if Michael has unconsciously invented a father figure who represented the qualities he longed for but never experienced. She said nothing about what baby Michael may have missed in a mother.

Chapter 10

"If you are not too long, I will wait here for you all my life."

—Oscar Wilde

As a child, Michael could not be expected to know how to mend himself or his family. He did not learn about receiving and giving love. What he learned was how to defend against threatened pain and punishment and shaming. He learned how to lie, manipulate, lash out, and disappear. He was a chronic runaway and spent most of his time on the streets. Older and bigger boys often bullied him and his younger brother. He resolved to stop it. The knife he started carrying as a teenager made him feel powerful. Even though he was not physically imposing, an intimidating presence was forged from Michael's athletic physique, street sense, and bravado.

Word spread that Michael Anderson was dangerous and fearless. Fighting, intimidation, and stealing became his pastime. They gave him a peculiar sense of status and identity for the first time in his life. Stealing cars became Michael's favorite crime—narcotic and felicitous amusement that brought him fleeting relief from sadness and confusion. A new Michael Anderson, the persona he would carry into adulthood, was emerging from little Michael's efforts to keep himself emotionally safe. Fifty-five years later, Michael described his adolescence "as a joyride through life, with a hedonistic mind-set, no understanding of who people were, no concept of consequences, and no empathy for other people's pain, insecurity, or shortcomings."

His larcenous habits caused Michael to spend parts of his fourteenth and fifteenth year at an Illinois juvenile facility, the St. Charles School and Home for Boys. Opened in December 1904, the boys' home sat on 901 acres of farmland west of St. Charles, Illinois. Its purpose was to provide delinquent boys with a strong education in both "intellectual and vocational studies" so that once released they could live a life of "usefulness." Soon after the school opened, it was proclaimed by the local newspaper as the "greatest institution of its kind, in ground plans and scope of possibilities, that has ever been attempted in America, if not in the known world." The school's layout was based on a system of individual residential units referred to as "cottages." Each cottage housed approximately forty boys and had a house mother and father who served as guardians. The intention was to create a "home-like environment" for the boys.

The institution experienced a history of financial challenges that adversely affected correctional staffing, education programming, and building maintenance. The correctional philosophy on which the institution had built its reputation was not matched by the lived reality of the young residents. Some were selected for especially brutal interventions because they were likely to resist or oppose rules and authority. Michael earned the respect of many boys who he would later connect with on the streets. It was these boys who dubbed him "Iron Mike" because of his ironclad defiance of authority and his fondness for weightlifting. The name was to follow Michael from prison to prison, even to the Washington State Penitentiary.

"Iron Mike" once escaped the boys' home for a few days. He was caught and placed in isolation. It was a tiny unadorned cell where he spent long hours looking out the small steel-barred window at a Ferris wheel located in a valley some distance from the boys' home. He remembers the exact day because it was June 3, 1968, his fifteenth birthday. The lonely boy was about to enter his sixteenth year estranged from his family, without skills beyond those that served his criminal objectives, and impervious to mainstream values and expectations by which society would judge him. However, an auspicious encounter awaited him, a bright spot on the horizon that he could not predict or foresee as he watched the Ferris wheel's relentless rotation from his sad little cell. He was about to meet Dee, a remarkable young woman who would see in Michael something sacred and eternal. She would change the course of his life, and he would change hers, but in neither case would it be easy or painless.

In 1968, Dee was fifteen years old, pretty, smart, and obedient. Boys noticed her. She lived with her single mother in Phoenix, Illinois, a small mostly African American community about ten miles south of Chicago. Dee's mother was religious, strict, and law-abiding. She belonged to an evangelical religious sect and required her daughter to conform to the group's expectations and values. Dee was prohibited from dating. During the school year, she was expected to come straight home after school to help with household chores and do homework.

THE LIFER AND THE LAWYER

On a windy October afternoon in 1968, Dee decided to stop at a local soda fountain frequented by teenagers who lived in Dee's neighborhood. She planned to buy an ice cream and then continue her walk home from school. Kids loitered and smoked on the sidewalk outside the storefront. This was not Dee's crowd and she did not dawdle or respond to the flirtatious utterances directed her way as she entered the shop and moved toward the ice cream counter. Just inside the doorway, she looked to the right and froze.

A strikingly good-looking boy was perched over a juke box surveying the music selections. He was severe in demeanor, almost fierce in the energy he projected across the room. He glanced up at Dee, their eyes locked, and Dee was instantly overcome by a powerful and ineffable understanding that this man would change her life. He was manifestly a bad boy, but Dee didn't care.

Almost fifty years later, Dee described the initial encounter: "I remember it like it was yesterday. I entered the shop, and my eyes immediately gravitated to this beautiful and imposing young man. He looked at me and my entire being started vibrating. I had never had a boyfriend, had never even been on a date. I was not a flirt and did not talk to strange boys. But I was a strong Christian, even at fifteen, and I knew in that moment that God intended this young man and me to spend our lives together."

Michael's memory of meeting Dee is more nuanced. He was in Phoenix because his mother and stepfather had moved to the town to escape Chicago's inner-city decay. He had just been released after serving nine months in the St. Charles Boys' Home.

Michael was struck by Dee's beauty and the fact that she was not intimidated by him despite his reputation. She was so different from him, yet similar. She had an aura, a presence, that he found alluring and intriguing. Dee was not at all forward, she made no advances, and did not respond to Michael's flirtatious overtures. Still, her eyes let him know her interest. He set out to find her address and, when a mutual friend disclosed the information, Michael marched over to Dee's house, knocked on the door, and, after introducing himself, asked Dee's mother if he might spend some time with her daughter. The mother said it was not a good time. Michael said he would be back, and he meant it. In time the two adolescents were able to see each other without impediments and they fell in love.

Dee grew close to Michael's mother, who welcomed Dee into her life. Shortly after Dee and Michael started seeing one another, a fickle Michael invited an old girlfriend to his mom's house. Abigail admonished him firmly, declaring, "Michael, don't bring that girl home. Dee is going to be my daughter-in-law!"

Dee became pregnant and delivered their first child, Nina, on October 31, 1969, a beautiful little girl who blessed Michael with sensibilities he had never known. He held Nina and felt the rush of emotion, the bond, the desire to protect, the tenderness of spirit that comes with a new baby. Her entry into his life was also the cause of pain and guilt that lingers to this day because, in the end, Nina grew up without a full-time dad, the very thing that had caused such emptiness and dysfunction in Michael's own life.

By November, Michael was back at St. Charles Boys Home for stealing one more of many cars. His crimes had become so reckless and self-destructive that he seemed to be unconsciously inviting arrest and imprisonment, as though that was the only strategy available to get the structure and guidance he needed. He would break into houses, steal stereo equipment, throw the stolen goods in the back end of a stolen car, speed down the street with no driver's license, a gun under the seat, waiting for the police to drive by, almost daring them to stop him, knowing full well what would happen when they did.

When he was sent up to the boys' home this time, however, he had new visitors—his new baby and her mother.

Michael got out of the boys' home in 1970. His plan, as always, was to do what made him feel good. He spent the next year honing his criminal skills on the streets of Chicago. His mother characterized this as the beginning of a new way of being for Michael, a lifestyle based on the assumption that his "home" was jail or prison from which he would periodically be released for brief "vacations," during which he would commit new crimes that would cause him to be returned "home."

He often floated from place to place, but he spent the night of May 30, 1971 and part of the following day at Dee's apartment with a very pregnant Dee and their seventeen-month-old infant daughter. It was a magical time. Almost fifty years have passed but Dee remembers the sweetness, the mutual expressions of affection, the gentle touches and shared dreams about their future. And the music. We all know that music evokes memories of special moments and people. It removes the distance between emotion and time. In our busy lives, if we should stop and listen, if we should savor a special song that is the portal to the moment of early love, let it wash over us and seep deeply into the cracks of our psyche's guarded interior, we might reconstruct the moment.

They had listened to Marvin Gaye's "What's Going On" and the Temptations' "Just My Imagination." Michael then did something completely out of character. The Temptations' "My Girl" was playing, and he took his expectant girlfriend by the hand, encircled her full waist with his other hand, and twirled her tenderly around the small apartment in a slow dance that affirmed she was, at that moment and forever, Michael's girl.

He was not there later that same day when Dee's water broke and she went to the hospital to deliver their son, Dwayne. Michael had been arrested for murder and was being booked about the time his son was delivered. Dee did not see Michael again for almost two years.

Chapter 11

"No matter where you go, there you are."

—Confucius

Because of his criminal history, Michael was often charged with crimes he did not commit as well as those he did commit. He spent thirteen months in the Cook County Jail waiting to stand trial on the murder charge. Additional charges were added when he and another inmate, Fatboy Watkins, attempted to escape by breaking a glass window and threatening a guard with a glass shard. Eventually, Michael beat the murder charge when a Cook County jury acquitted him after hearing overwhelming evidence that he was elsewhere at the time of the crime and had been wrongly and maliciously targeted by local police simply because of his reputation.

By 1974, Michael was doing time at the Illinois Statesville Penitentiary in Joliet after having been arrested and convicted for attempted murder and robbery, crimes he did commit. He had robbed a tavern and shot an employee. The incident occurred in broad daylight across the street from a police station in a small Chicago suburb. The tavern's silent alarm had been activated, and Michael was quickly apprehended. He and his partner, Herman, had run out into the street and immediately taken off their disguises. People recognized them.

Why did Michael shoot the tavern employee? Did he think about the employee's family, his life, his pain? Why did he try to rob a tavern in broad daylight, a bar located across the street from a police station? And what did he think might happen when he took off his disguise in a community where he was known? After years of recklessness, this incident may have been the pinnacle of self-defeating, destructive behavior. By this time, Michael had two children and was twenty years old. What could possibly have been going on in his head? What was he feeling?

Forty-five years later, Michael answered these and other questions while he sat quietly in an austere visitation room at the Airway Heights Correctional Center just outside of Spokane. I was his visitor, his lawyer, and his inquisitor. Who was the tavern employee you shot? *A maintenance man.* Why did you shoot him? *He refused to stay put.* Where was he hit? *I shot him through the chest.* You had Dee and two children. What in God's name were you thinking?

Michael said nothing for several moments. He was pensive, looked away, and then said: "I wasn't thinking. More importantly, I wasn't feeling anything. Today, and for many years, I have wondered about the man's family, his children, the physical pain and financial hardship I caused. But, at the time, he was just in my way and I thought nothing of it. I was empty."

"But Michael," I said, "I remember feeling empty and alone and confused as a kid. But I didn't rob and shoot people."

"George, I don't think you understand," Michael replied. "When I said I was empty, I mean *literally* I was empty. There was nothing there. It wasn't like I was feeling a moment of depression, or a few hours or days of angst and loneliness and frustration. When you felt those things as a child or young person, there were ways to get beyond the feeling, to start feeling better. You probably had goals, there were probably expectations people had for you. There may have been people who you could talk to or who would reach out to you. You probably had healthy habits and ways of acting that you had been taught for many years. Maybe you had people you looked up to and wanted to impress. And I bet you liked yourself. When I shot that poor man and did a thousand other things, I felt empty, and there was nothing there to replace the emptiness. I just didn't care about anything, including myself."

"What about Dee and your children?" I asked. "You had feelings for them."

"I did. But somehow those feelings never got connected to me in a way that made me feel confident or like I was a real father. Of course, I had no ability to analyze anything at the time, but looking back it seems like there were two people. There was me, this low-life criminal who felt angry and empty. And there was this other guy who loved Dee and the children, but who was not real. I know now, of course, that one of the reasons I felt empty and disconnected is because there was nothing guiding me except for random, egocentric thoughts. I had no anchor, no connection with God, and no appreciation for other people's pain. I had no empathy and could not have even told you what the word meant."

After his arrest for the tavern robbery and shooting, he was incarcerated in a local city jail from which he promptly escaped with a cellmate, whose girlfriend smuggled in a hacksaw. He was arrested the next day at his aunt's home in Chicago. The court accepted his guilty plea and he was sentenced to confinement in the Illinois State Penitentiary, where he spent the next three years and three months before being paroled. You could not describe Michael's life as lucky at this point, but he was very lucky the tavern employee survived.

Michael had two children and a girlfriend, but he did not know how to love them. His life was broken, and he was on a trajectory leading to permanent incarceration or death unless he could heal. But the state penitentiary was not a therapeutic environment. It was one of the toughest prisons in the country and Michael's goal was to survive. He also wanted to develop influence and contacts that could be exploited after his parole. By his own account, he learned nothing in his three years at the Joliet penitentiary except how to improve on the nefarious skills he had cultivated on the streets and in other institutions. By this time, everyone—prison officials and fellow convicts—were calling him Iron Mike.

However, an incident occurred during his captivity at Joliet that created in him an emotional current that ran counter to his normal way of being in the world. A fellow prisoner who was a good friend was the victim of an assault that almost killed him. Another prisoner plunged a six-inch piece of steel through the friend's neck. The bloody incident and possible loss of a friend upset Michael in a way that caused him to question whether his lifestyle and compulsions could ever give him any lasting satisfaction. He wondered if there might be a way to live without hurting people. The notion seemed almost impossible to test in the chaos and danger of prison life. He would not seriously revisit the idea for many years.

When he was released from the penitentiary in March 1977, Michael lived with Dee and the children in an apartment Dee had rented in South Chicago's famous Altgeld Gardens. This was the huge public housing project nicknamed Chicago's "toxic donut" because it had the highest concentration of hazardous waste sites in the United States. Shortly after Dee and Michael moved from Altgeld Gardens, a grassroots campaign was organized to clean up the area. Former President Barack Obama participated in this campaign during his early years as a local community organizer and wrote about his experience in his biography *Dreams of My Father*.

The "good" Michael, the one who was ephemeral, perhaps even imaginary, hoped he might settle down, work, and lead a normal life. By summer, however, the Michael who was an inveterate criminal was arrested for burglary in Harvey, Illinois, and taken to the Harvey City Jail. He sat in a small cell overcome by shame when his eyes wandered to a clock beyond the bars on a far wall. It was three in the afternoon, the time Michael had promised his two children he would take them to the park. He imagined their sad faces looking for him out the window of their apartment at Altgeld Gardens. They waited, as always, for the absent father who seemed destined to disappoint them. The image caused Michael to explode with pain, and he cried like he had never cried before, a powerful lament that came from deep inside him. As he cried, a great peace came over him, and he felt the presence of God.

He asked, "Is this you, God?" and prayed for a blessing that might change his life.

From that point forward, Michael continued to look for God's presence—always hoping for an earthshaking moment, a miracle, some indisputable proof of God's existence. For years and years, he kept an eye out. Eventually his life did change, but only after he fled Chicago and tried to escape his demons on the banks of the Columbia River in the remote desert of eastern Washington.

He was out of jail again and learned the police were looking to arrest him on new warrants. He and Dee decided to leave Illinois and start a new life out West. In October of 1977 they boarded Amtrak's venerable Empire Builder in Chicago and followed the Lewis and Clark trail to the small southeastern Washington town of Pasco—just across the Columbia River from Kennewick, and just downriver from Richland. It was another world. They had moved from the tough, congested streets of Chicago to an arid, sparsely populated plateau drained by a great river.

The Cascade Mountains run north and south through the center of Washington. Their eastern foothills drop gradually in elevation and become the Columbia Basin, a parched plateau that spreads east to Spokane and south from there to Walla Walla, Pasco, and Yakima. The Columbia River cuts a path from headwaters in British Columbia through central and eastern Washington basalt before the Columbia Gorge funnels the river to the Pacific Ocean along the Oregon-Washington border. The river's twentieth-century dams stopped the great salmon runs of the past but produced abundant electric power and irrigation for the entire Northwest. Before the great dams, there had been some irrigation along the river, but agriculture was predominantly dry land farming, mostly winter wheat. With the dams came water for peas and potatoes, onions, corn, mint, hay,

PART 2: DARKNESS

and hops; and fruit trees—apple, cherry, peach, and plum. The new millennium brought grapes, lots of grapes, which engendered a burgeoning wine industry and transformed much of the region into vast vineyards sprinkled with Tuscan-like wineries and chateaus, all nourished by water diverted from the great river's path to the sea.

Pasco was a small farm town throughout most of the late nineteenth and early twentieth centuries. The Northern Pacific Railroad put it on the map in the late 1800s, but the town was not much more than a crossroad in sparsely populated scab-lands. However, the population of the entire region exploded during World War II due to the location of a Naval Air Station in Pasco, and the establishment of the Hanford Atomic Energy Works in nearby Richland. By the time Michael came to Pasco in 1977, it was a quiet, mostly white, and unofficially segregated town of some 17,000 people. African Americans, who had once been attracted to Pasco by railroad work, comprised less than 5 percent of the population and lived mostly in a discrete community on the town's east side. There was also a burgeoning Latino population that came to the region for employment opportunities in agriculture.

Pasco was not Chicago, and life in this radically different place began well enough for Michael and Dee. They rented an apartment and obtained minimum wage jobs. Michael worked across the river from Pasco, in Kennewick, as a school district groundskeeper. Dee worked as a retail clerk at a local hardware store. They sent for their two children, nine-year-old Nina and six-year-old Dwayne, who had been left temporarily in the custody of Dee's mother in Illinois. The children flew into Pendleton, Oregon, about seventy miles south of Pasco. They had barely glimpsed their father during the brief times he was not in prison or jail and they were elated to know the whole family would be together. The family's reunion was jubilant, everyone in tears, and the ride back to Pasco, across the Columbia at Umatilla, through wheat fields and sagebrush and dust, was filled with storytelling and expectation. The children's new home had been methodically readied for their arrival; there were bikes, toys, and clothing and furnished bedrooms. They all put Chicago behind them and tried to visualize a happy and stable new life.

Chapter 12

"The Darkness is a dangerous place. It has the ability, the power, to take you where you do not want to go, or keep you there longer than you want to stay..."

—Michael Anderson

Unfortunately, Michael's vision was occluded by the restive and unappeasable impulses that had followed him West. Sometimes he wondered what it might be like to come out from the shadows, to live with pride and confidence, to bare his life to the world, his soul to God, without fear or guile. This abstraction was manifest everywhere he looked. There were people, happy people, white and black, going about their lives without being dominated by uncontrollable and dangerous desires.

Now was the time to transform his life. He hoped his new circumstances would lead to healthy behaviors and choices. Dee encouraged him. He tried to imitate the look and deportment of people who seemed normal, but it was impossible because he had no idea what "normal" felt like and because he had never experienced contentment. The habits, instincts, and neural pathways that led to empathy and intimacy were nonexistent. He could not appreciate other people's feelings when his own feelings were so inaccessible and muddled. Darkness consumed him, attracted him, nurtured him. The picture of love, the images that populated his mind when he thought of his family, were real. But he did not really know love, did not know the feeling of love in action. He was alone, disconnected and incomplete. The idea that he could be a storybook dad and intimate partner was as weightless and impermanent as a daydream about being a movie star.

Michael's compulsions soon steered him back to selfish, hurtful behavior. He wandered the streets of Pasco looking for trouble. Occasionally, he would see a sheriff's vehicle that transported prisoners from the local county jail to the state penitentiary in Walla Walla. He had a preternatural sense that one day he would take a ride in that vehicle. The predator in him discovered that crime was even more tempting in eastern Washington than it had been in Chicago. People were less guarded than big city folks and Michael was quick to take advantage.

Within a few months of his arrival in Pasco, local police came to his home to arrest him for armed robbery of a local Safeway store. They suspected him of other crimes as well. He violently resisted and managed to flee into quiet nearby neighborhoods. He was finally caught and handcuffed after a fight, ironically, in the backyard of a local law enforcement officer's home. The Franklin County Jail became his new home as he awaited trial on charges of robbery and resisting arrest.

Frustration and self-loathing overwhelmed Michael as he sat alone in yet *another* miserable jail cell. Self-loathing damaged him in complicated ways. He believed he deserved constant punishment, which, of course, became self-fulfilling. He pursued behaviors that affirmed the unsalvageable person he believed himself to be. He was caught in a loop and could not change. It was futile to fight against what he thought was his own nature.

He formed an escape plan. The first plan failed when a jail guard foiled his attempt to steal jail keys. Sheriff's deputies beat him and dumped him in an isolation cell for a month. He was placed back in the general population after promising he would no longer try to escape. He immediately began formulating a new plan. Weeks later, he assaulted a guard, locked him in a cell, and made his way with three other inmates through a series of jail doors whose electronic locking codes he had closely observed and memorized.

The escape was successful. It was a cold, gray, and rainy day in April 1978. He was now a young black escapee on the loose in the inhospitable streets of a mostly white community in America's inland Northwest. Franklin County deputies and Pasco police detectives and patrolmen dispersed throughout the city in dogged pursuit. They visited Dee. She and the children knew nothing about Michael's whereabouts, but they were kept under surveillance. Detectives had previously impounded Michael's burgundy Ford Galaxy 500 and the car remained in police custody because Dee could not afford to pay the impound fees. Detectives drove the vehicle slowly back and forth in front of Dee's apartment.

* * * *

Following his escape, Michael had hidden for hours in a boat parked behind a home a few blocks from the jail. Then he'd made his way to the apartment of an acquaintance, a street hustler named Goldie, who gave him a .38-caliber pistol, hollow-point bullets, and a shoulder holster. Goldie was well known to the police so he told Michael about a friend's house where he would be safe. They set out at night in Goldie's car with Michael lying on the back seat. A police car passed and slowed. Goldie sped up and then stopped briefly after they rounded a corner. Michael bailed out and buried himself in nearby bushes. The police cruiser passed, and the fugitive waited breathlessly in the darkness. Finally, he made his way on foot to the house Goldie said would be a safehouse.

The house was not a secure hideout. Goldie's friend had a wife and children who had all been alerted to Anderson's escape and notoriety. They were terrified. They had no choice but to give the anxious and armed fugitive sanctuary for the night, but the next morning one of the children informed her schoolteacher that a man who had escaped from jail was hiding in her house. Law enforcement surrounded the property, but not before Michael climbed into an attic space that was only accessible from an opening outside the house on the roof above the soffit. The police searched the house in vain. When they left, Anderson crept down from the roof and reentered the house. He waited until nightfall, then slipped out a back door and picked his way through back alleys and backyards avoiding barking dogs and homes without landscaping. Cold, tired, and desperate, Michael wanted shelter and a place to hide until police activity subsided and he could figure out his next move.

Of course, the idea of a refuge was magical thinking on Michael's part. He imagined he was running from the police and needed a hideout, that that would be a solution. He did not know he was running from himself, had always been running from himself, and would continue to do so until he could feel something more than pain and worthlessness.

The home he selected was typical of single-family, middle-class Pasco houses built in the 1950s. It was a nicely maintained frame construction with several bedrooms, mature landscaping, and a basement. Watching from a perch behind the garage, Michael impulsively decided to enter the house when he observed that the back door was ajar. He had no idea who occupied the home. When all the lights went out, he crept across the backyard and silently squeezed through the unlocked door. Just inside were stairs leading to the basement. He tiptoed down and let his eyes adjust to the dim light. There was a vacant bedroom, another room furnished with a pool table and fully stocked bar, and a laundry room. He drank some

PART 2: DARKNESS

wine and began to warm. His breathing calmed. He stopped shivering and waited. The upstairs was quiet.

Michael felt the same as the six-year-old boy who killed the kittens. His mother had told him after that incident that they would soon hear the sirens of police cars and Michael would be taken away. When the police never came, his mother let him know they were waiting and might still come at any time. Eighteen years later, police sirens resounded through Pasco's staid residential neighborhoods. The sound was muffled but Michael knew there were lots of angry police in relentless pursuit.

He had no intention of contacting or harming the family members who slept innocently in bedrooms above him. He had no plan and no specific goals. He had navigated the darkness in pure survival mode, alert and agile, driven by instinct and primal energy, selfish and amoral, oblivious to what the dawn might bring. He knew only one thing: at least for this one night, the police would not find him. He crawled under the pool table and slept.

* * * *

It was morning. Anderson's name and photo dominated local television news. Viewers were warned to be on the lookout for a twenty-four-year-old black male, a convicted felon from Chicago who was wanted for armed robbery and escape from the local jail.

The family awoke and went through its rituals as spring sunlight streamed across the kitchen and dining room. The children laughed and teased. The dad, Mr. Carlson, talked about the upcoming Seattle SuperSonics-Los Angeles Lakers playoff series, and Mrs. Carlson hoped to score well at her afternoon bowling tournament. After breakfast, the children went to school and the dad left for work. Michael heard constant footsteps above. He remained hidden and waited. Mrs. Carlson was a stay-at-home mom and her day was filled with household chores. She came down into the basement several times to access the laundry room. In the afternoon, Anderson heard her talking on the phone with a friend about going bowling. When she left the house, he shot upstairs and eagerly consumed a sandwich and a glass of milk.

Some particle of compassion for Dee and the children momentarily eclipsed Michael's egocentric thinking and he called the police station to announce that he would turn himself in if the authorities promised to drop pending welfare fraud charges against Dee. The dispatcher assured him the appropriate officials would discuss the proposal and instructed Michael to call back. He knew a follow-up phone call would be traced. He made other calls trying to arrange a secure hideaway.

Michael was back in the basement pondering his next move. The faint downstairs light was comforting. Twilight was approaching and he hoped for a moonless, black night that would conceal him and aid his escape. The forces that had ruled Michael since childhood were powerful and he had grown to understand literal and metaphoric darkness to be inseparable. His thoughts were dark, and he lived in the shadows, restless, alert, aimless, and lost.

It occurred to him that he might steal a car. He had stolen plenty of cars. The planning and execution produced endorphins that countered feelings of emptiness. Yes, the high quickly went away, especially on those occasions when he was thrown in jail, but it made sense in his present circumstances. There were few options.

Mrs. Carlson had returned home from bowling and the children were home from school. Not yet finished with the laundry, she came downstairs unexpectedly. Michael quickly moved from the pool room into a bedroom. In the basement's dim light, the woman heard something and glimpsed a movement. She called out to the person she assumed was one of her sons. And then she entered the bedroom where Michael was wedged behind the door desperately hoping the woman might return to her laundry chores. The house was quiet, the basement bedroom deadly quiet. And dark. Michael lunged for the woman. She screamed. He grabbed her and she resisted. They fought. Michael reached for the gun in his shoulder holster and whipped the pistol across the forty-seven-year-old mother's face. Mrs. Carlson collapsed on the floor and he kicked her until she fell silent. Blood flowed from her face, down her cheeks and onto her blouse.

Michael ran up the stairs to prevent the children from raising an alarm. Two of the Carlson sons and a neighbor boy sat on the living room floor sorting newspapers. Just then, Mr. Carlson walked through the front door. Anderson instantly put the gun to his temple and said: "Get on the floor or I will shoot you."

He gagged the five captives, including the mother, and bound their hands and feet with torn bed sheets. At some point he seized thirty dollars contained in the father's wallet.

PART 2: DARKNESS

This is not how things were supposed to turn out. He had hoped to slip out of the house into the night undetected. He certainly had not intended to harm anyone. Now, he would have to leave the Carlsons bound and immobile and try to make his way back to Goldie's place before the family was discovered. Goldie would help—he knew Pasco, had been born in Pasco. Michael would let things calm down, then steal a car and get out of town. Darkness was finally blanketing eastern Washington and would provide the necessary cover.

And then the telephone rang. Michael quickly removed the woman's gag and ordered her to answer and act normal. She did and reported it was a neighbor complaining that the newspaper had not been delivered that afternoon by one of the children who had a daily paper route. There was then a knock on the front door. Anderson froze and ordered the mother to peek out the window. She informed him that there were two men at the door who she did not recognize.

The men at the door soon departed. Anderson was now panicked, and he impulsively ordered the woman to get her car keys and coat. They were going to take a drive, Michael in the backseat with his gun, the woman driving. They left the house. Bloody and bruised, her emotions raw, her face swollen, the woman obligingly walked to the driveway, opened the car door, and climbed behind the wheel of the family car. Terrified about her own prospects, she was nonetheless relieved to drive this marauding stranger away from her loved ones who remained bound and gagged in the house.

Franklin County law enforcement and Pasco City Police were eager to end the drama. The jail escape embarrassed them. A jail guard had been assaulted and humiliated. They would be incensed when they discovered the escape had led to an audacious and violent home invasion. The full measure of government power and resources would be mobilized to capture or kill the beast.

Once the fugitive and his hostage crossed the old bridge that spanned the Columbia River from Pasco to Kennewick, they were out of Franklin County and into Benton County. The Franklin County crimes were over. The Benton County crimes were about to begin.

Chapter 13

"I was at the end of my road. All of my dysfunction from early adolescence had culminated in darkness that placed me at death's door..."

—MICHAEL ANDERSON

In the 1970s, Kennewick, like Pasco, was still a manageable small town. It was easy to navigate and culturally uncomplicated. It had a middle class 1950s quality overlaid with an icing of new money, disco, and drugs. Latin American cocaine and black tar heroin had entered the culture, but except for a few shopping malls and the construction of fancy homes on the city's south and west sides, Kennewick looked much the same as it had in earlier generations. There were long tree-lined streets and quiet neighborhoods. Schools, parks, and a small downtown dominated its core, but apartments and strip malls stretched for miles to the west. This was before social media. Young people still cruised the town's main drags and collected at popular fast food joints. Mexican immigrants attracted to the area by farm work added an element of diversity, but African Americans were a rare sight on the streets or in the schools.

Kennewick joins Richland and Pasco to form the metropolitan area known as the Tri-Cities. The three cities owe their existence to farming fed by the Columbia River watershed, the Northern Pacific Railroad, and the nearby Hanford Nuclear Reservation that produced the plutonium used in the bomb, "Fat Man," that destroyed Nagasaki at the end of World War II. Agriculture and nuclear projects had attracted big federal money since the 1940s. The federal investment today is for environmental clean-up rather than for bombs and energy, but that first big bomb will always be a part of the Tri-City brand. The towns are politically and culturally conservative—local folks appreciate Seattle football and baseball and shopping, but they vote differently than Seattle voters.

Michael Anderson forced his captive to drive him over the Columbia River from Pasco into Kennewick for two reasons: the road to Seattle went through Kennewick, and he needed money. Ironically, Michael was the first black man to work for the Kennewick School District as a groundskeeper. He knew the city because, for a few months, he had traveled from school to school to maintain lawns and common areas. Just weeks earlier, he had everything he and Dee had hoped for when they moved to Pasco—a job, a home, and a new start. Now, firmly ensnared by the familiar emotions that ruled him in Illinois, he drove the streets of Kennewick as an escaped felon, in a stolen car, with a bloody hostage, fleeing from city and county law enforcement. He was armed and planning a robbery.

There were some big stores in Kennewick that were likely to contain piles of cash. Michael would wait until closing time to attempt the robbery. He ordered his hostage to drive around Kennewick to kill time. He knew at some point the woman's husband and children would be discovered and the woman's car would become the object of a massive search. In addition to money, he needed to find another vehicle.

* * * *

As 9 PM approached, Michael decided to rob the Giant T, a big all-purpose store located about two blocks from the house in which I was raised on Kennewick Avenue and just across the street from Fruitland Elementary School where I had attended first through sixth grades. The store was located on a huge patch of land that, in my youth, had been one of the largest single grape vineyards in the world. The vineyard no longer existed, but its footprint left an odd, partially developed open space in the middle of town.

They parked in a remote corner of the Giant T parking lot and waited in darkness for closing time. Rain pounded the windshield. The woman's heart pounded too. She was disabled now, mute and inert, paralyzed by shock and her fear of what was to come. Just before 9 PM, Anderson abandoned any pretense of humanity. He forced himself on Mrs. Carlson, hoping the act might alter the all-encompassing bleakness, might mitigate his feelings of isolation and despair, might infuse and invigorate him with power and confidence.

They were in a locked car at the back of a big empty parking lot on a moonless night. This rape of a trembling, blood-stained forty-seven-year-old mother and wife easily marked the deepest point of Michael's iniquitous descent. Mrs. Carlson was consumed by fear and, at the same time, almost beyond fear. Knowing she might die, she intentionally refocused from worldly cares to something more infinite. She whimpered and turned her mind to prayer, repeating words that invited the Lord to walk with her. Michael had second thoughts and ended the assault before completion. He apologized, his words a pathetic and confused attempt to diminish the little bit of guilt that penetrated his cold, hard heart. She thanked him and pleaded, "Please, just don't hurt me anymore."

Michael ordered Mrs. Carlson to get into the trunk of the car. She obeyed. He locked the trunk and then stealthily entered the back door of the Giant T just as the manager was locking the front doors.

Only a few customers and employees remained in the store. When an employee ventured into the back room, Anderson shoved his gun in the employee's face and ordered him to locate the manager. Michael forced the manager to open two locked safes. The yield was $10,000 in cash. Two store employees, excluding the manager, were locked in the store's attached pharmacy. Anderson made sure the employees heard him talking about his intention to head north to Spokane. Then he marched the store manager to the parking lot at gunpoint and located the manager's car, a newer model station wagon in good condition. Michael assumed the police would be looking for the woman's car. He ordered the Giant T manager to drive him to Seattle in the station wagon. Fearing Mrs. Carlson might suffocate in the trunk of her car, he opened the trunk and transferred her to the station wagon.

They headed west through Richland onto state highway 240 and into the dark eastern Washington desert. This was the desolate Hanford Nuclear Reservation controlled by the federal government as a site for nuclear reactors that produced the plutonium for most of the 60,000 weapons built for America's nuclear arsenal. Today, there is no such production. There is, however, remnant radioactive waste that will last for thousands of years.

They first stopped for gas. The store manager filled the gas tank and might easily have escaped. But he feared for the other hostage's safety and stayed with the vehicle in the hope that he could persuade Anderson to stay calm and not hurt anyone. Years later, Anderson described the Giant T store manager as "a real man, a true hero" who put himself at risk to help another person.

The trio disappeared into blackness, the overcast sky fused with a bleak desert horizon and inky asphalt highway. They were on a two-lane road with little traffic. No one spoke. The store manager drove and struggled to control his fear as he mulled over options for escape and tried to gauge

Anderson's intentions. He wondered if behind the fugitive's nervous and menacing front, there might be some capacity to feel compassion, some empathetic quality the manager could probe and exploit to avoid violent injury or death. Michael sat in the back of the car holding his gun in silence. He watched for police vehicles.

There was no real plan. He had money. Perhaps he could buy a plane ticket and fly to some warm place where he could hide out in comfort and solitude. As he stared into the night, there was a barely discernible twinkling of lights in the far distance to the north, lights that illuminated places that were unknown and inaccessible to Anderson.

He was on a long dark road that had no turns.

Chapter 14

"I looked into the drawn guns of two officers in full tactical gear, one low, one high. Everything slowed down and became surreal, misty. I knew I was at death's doorway and would now reap the rewards of darkness."

—Michael Anderson

The station wagon was deep in the desert approaching the Wanapum Dam on the Columbia River, as the river ran south from British Columbia. They were now in central Washington heading toward the Cascade mountain range and Seattle to the west. There were no cars on the road and, apart from enormous electric lines, no signs of life. It had not always been so. The Wanapum Indians traditionally lived in this area. The tribe is almost lost to history. "Wanapum" means "river people"—people who had roamed the area since prehistoric times relying on salmon to sustain them and their way of life. Houses were built along the river valleys, houses made from the thick green stems of the tule plants that grew in the marshes. Tribal people cut hundreds of petroglyphs into the basalt cliffs scattered throughout Columbia Plateau. A Wanapum chief, Cutssahnem, greeted Lewis and Clark in 1805 and, according to Captain Clark, the tribe welcomed the expedition with enthusiasm and food. The Wanapum people were pacifists. Instead of participating in armed conflicts, the people prayed. The tribe never fought white settlers and signed no treaty. Their religion notwithstanding, the Wanapums were no match for Manifest Destiny: their historic lands were appropriated by white settlers; their homes and salmon runs flooded by the great dams of the Snake and Columbia River system; their numbers diminished by disease; and their bloodline diluted, diverted, and mostly fused into the melting pot of modern American culture.

Anderson knew nothing of this history and wanted only to get through this desolate land quickly without being spotted by law enforcement. He and his hostages made good time and soon intersected Interstate 90, the major highway that bisects Washington and affords travelers an expeditious route over the Cascade Mountains to Seattle. The car crossed the Columbia River at Vantage, just north of Wanapum Dam, in the middle of the state, and Michael was able to make out the outline of craggy peaks on the western horizon. They started up the foothills towards Ellensburg. The Interstate bypassed the town and began to climb into forested mountains periodically broken by scenic valleys. This was quintessential high plateau cowboy country and Michael almost started to enjoy himself as the dawn approached. The spectacular landscape bore little resemblance to the asphalt life he had known on the streets of south Chicago.

Soon they came to Snoqualmie Pass, dominated by high mountains north and south of the highway. It was too late in the season for skiing, but Michael gazed in wonder at sculpted and manicured ski slopes and the chair lifts that that ran vertically up the mountains just south of the highway. He could not imagine the people or lifestyle associated with a pastime that involved spending winter days outdoors in exotic mountain resorts sprinkled with high-end housing and fancy restaurants. He was certain of one thing—such a lifestyle was reserved for privileged people. Michael would never ski, never slide fluidly and freely down sparkling slopes on a sunlit day, never feel the invigorating flush of mountain wind against his face, never sip a hot buttered rum by the fire in an upscale bar at the end of an exquisitely exhausting day. He knew it was more likely he would spend the rest of his life asking a prison guard for permission to pee.

The end of the dramatic affair unfolded in Seattle. They traversed the floating bridge from Mercer Island into Seattle across Lake Washington, where Bill Gates and other technology kings would someday build fabulous homes. Michael felt relief that they had made it without incident. The Tri-Cities were far behind. Now there was the difficult matter of what to do with the hostages. He could not just let them go. They drove around the city in the early morning hours while Michael pondered the problem, his hostages terrified that he might settle on the worst possible solution.

They drove by the Kingdome where the Seattle Seahawks and Seattle Mariners played. The Giant T manager navigated light downtown traffic, anxiously trying to formulate a survival strategy that would appeal to his unpredictable captor. As the car headed north, the three desperate occupants sunk into silent reveries about their respective lives, families, and uncertain futures. Finally, the Giant T manager suggested a plan. He would use his credit card to rent a hotel room where Michael could tie up the hostages and make his getaway. The manager knew of a conveniently located hotel right off Interstate 5 in the University District north of downtown.

Michael had developed a measure of trust for the man because of the discursive and friendly way they had chatted as they approached Seattle. The manager had promised not to obstruct his plans, whatever they might be. He asked Michael to be gentle with the woman. He wanted what was best for all three. Michael's frayed and fatigued brain interpreted the manager's good will as a sign the manager wanted him to get away, a perception that was reinforced by the fact that during the Giant T robbery, the manager, without coaxing, had volunteered the existence and location of a second safe.

Anderson agreed to the plan and everyone enjoyed a momentary break in the tension. The group made their way to the University Inn next to the freeway on 45th Street. He dictated how the check-in would go down and reminded his hostages he was still armed. The stress mounted again as the Giant T manager approached the hotel clerk at the front desk. Michael alternated watching Mrs. Carlson—who remained in the car—and monitoring the manager and the hotel clerk. He was positioned at a discreet distance near the hotel's front entrance, armed with his loaded .38-caliber pistol, and could not hear the Giant T manager furtively alert the hotel clerk about the hostage situation. The self-possessed clerk calmly arranged for a room and politely directed his curious collection of guests, including the trembling and terrified, blood-streaked mother of three, to the elevator. He then called the police. Looking back on this incident from the perspective of many years, Anderson viewed the hotel clerk in the same light that he viewed the store manager—a hero who handled a dangerous situation with courage, intelligence, and composure.

Once in the room, Anderson tore up some sheets, tied his hostages to a bed, got some candy bars from the reception area, and reserved a morning flight bound for Los Angeles. He periodically let his hostages use the bathroom and freshen up. Michael was nervous. He went back downstairs to the reception desk to see if anything was amiss. The clerk was on the phone but immediately hung up after saying, "I have a customer. Yes, he is here right now." Michael could not be sure who was on the other end of the conversation. He returned to the hotel room.

The flight to LA was scheduled for later in the morning and it was too early to leave for the airport. He waited impatiently, pacing, and periodically putting his ear to the door. His captives were told to stay quiet. The room was at the end of a hall somewhat isolated from other guest rooms. They occasionally heard noise in the hallway.

What he did not know is that the Seattle SWAT team had surrounded the hotel and two team members in full tactical gear were stationed in the hallway outside Michael's door. That was the bad news for Michael. The good news was that the SWAT team had no knowledge of who Michael was, where he was from, his prior record, the Pasco home invasion or Giant T robbery, or the fact that he was armed. Had these things been know, the team would almost certainly have killed Michael on the spot and the record of his short life would be entered and forgotten in law enforcement archives.

The horrific drama ended when Anderson finally left the room with the intention of grabbing a taxi and going to the airport to catch his flight to Los Angeles. He was immediately confronted in the hallway by two SWAT team members brandishing automatic weapons. They were poised, well-trained, confident, and determined. Anderson jumped into an alcove and pulled his pistol from the shoulder holster. A SWAT team officer approached and observed the pistol. He looked Anderson directly in the eye from close range. He spoke, firmly but calmly, and Anderson will never forget the words: "Drop your weapon and you will not die."

Michael felt the world, his life, the actions of the SWAT team, and all his memories slow from a sprint to a crawl. His life's trajectory was projected as a series of slow-motion images in his mind's eye. A mist filled the hotel hallway, and he sensed that powerful and dramatic forces were engaged in a surreal struggle. Suddenly the mist dispersed, and his reality sped up. He heard a SWAT member say, this time more loudly, "Drop the weapon!" It might have gone either way, but for some reason, a reason grounded in biology or the divine, Michael made the decision not to die. He dropped his pistol and was taken into custody.

The hostages were freed and given emergency medical assistance. They immediately called their respective families across the state. The beaten and bruised mother of three spent several days in a Seattle hospital.

Anderson gave a full and detailed confession to the police. He experienced fleeting relief as his mind and body unwound from the adrenaline-infused events that might easily have resulted in his death. Perhaps now that he was back in a controlled environment there could be some respite from acting out his dangerous and irrepressible impulses.

That was unlikely. From his experience doing hard time in hard prisons, he knew he was now facing a grim new reality. He knew that for a very long time there would be no deliverance from violence and danger in the dark and unforgiving world to which he would be sent—the world where a man's survival depended on his ability to hurt people.

Chapter 15

"Love is patient, love is kind . . . it is not easily angered . . . it keeps no record of wrongs . . . it always protects, always trusts, always hopes, always perseveres."

—1 Corinthians 3:4–8

Dee was devastated when Michael was arrested for robbing a Pasco Safeway store in January 1978. She loved Michael but she also knew all about his impulsiveness, his constant need for power and control, and the ways these compulsions produced bad decisions and criminal behavior. She had believed that Michael could truly change if he replaced the chaos and drama of his former life with relative peace and calm. Michael's robbery arrest shattered the family's hope that their move to Pasco might foster a new life and an opportunity for family stability. The Safeway robbery did not end Dee's hope for the future or her commitment to Michael, but it caused her to wonder how much more she could take. She prayed that Michael might not be required to do too much time on the robbery charge. She would support him this one last time. And wait, wait once again, for Michael to go to prison and come back home.

Dee's life with Michael had already been a stormy mix of passion, pain, and regret. She did not know the storm that awaited. She could not know Michael would escape from the local jail and launch a crime spree that would terrify people from Pasco to Seattle.

Why would an attractive young woman stay with a man like Michael when it was obvious he was addicted to destructive, antisocial patterns of behavior? Was it the fact that they had two children? Was she an example of an abused partner trapped in a cycle of emotional and physical violence, lacking in self-esteem, bereft of external support, and unable to visualize a way out? Did she depend on Michael for financial survival?

I had gotten to know Dee, and I probed for answers to such questions as I prepared to represent Michael before the parole board in 2018. She still lived in Pasco and had enjoyed a successful career employed by the Pasco

School District as a classroom aide working with students on reading skills, math, and test preparation. She had worked in that position since 1995. She had always worked. In Chicago, she had been a bank clerk. She worked for a hardware store, a nursing home, and daycare program in Pasco before her employment with the school district.

Her children were long since grown. They had graduated from Pasco High School. They now had their own families in distant cities. Dee's life was not without challenges, but it was faith-based, grounded, and focused on service to others. She worked, worshiped, and spent time with her grandchildren and great grandchildren when she could. And, every month, as she had for almost forty years, she drove to wherever Michael was incarcerated for extended family visits. There was no one prouder of Michael's commitment to Christ's teaching than Dee.

She was not a victim. Michael had not always been kind to her, much less a reliable partner. Neither had he been a loving, attentive father to their children. Even before he was sentenced to do time in the Illinois penitentiary, she had taken the advice of family and friends and cut off contact with Anderson. For almost five years, she had focused on her children, cultivated a relationship with another man, and tried to forget Anderson. The problem was that she loved him and could not erase him from her life. When he was released from the prison in Joliet, he contacted her, and she followed her heart. They resumed their relationship and began talking about creating a new life together. She was ecstatic that Michael was willing to make a clean start by moving to Pasco.

"It was April 1978 when Michael escaped from the Franklin County Jail and terrorized that poor family in Pasco," Dee remembered. "I could not believe it. I was not just shocked and disappointed, I was shattered. We had such hopes in coming to Pasco. Not just to put Chicago and Michael's past behind us, but to truly move forward in a righteous and godly way. Michael had gotten a job and was spending time with the children. We had a nice apartment and we were meeting new people. He was still distant and moody, but he had always been that way and I had learned to live with it. He did what he wanted to. I just hoped what he wanted to do had changed. He had a hard time expressing his feelings. He could go days without talking. Still, I felt that he cared for me and the children."

I asked, "When Michael was arrested in Seattle and returned to the Tri-Cities, what did he tell you?"

PART 2: DARKNESS

"He did not try to justify anything. He just said he was sorry, that his life was over, and that I should move on without him. He did not have the words to describe what caused him to do the things he did. I think there was a big part of him that operated almost like a different person, a person he did not understand and could not control. The Michael I knew, the man who was the father of my children, never hit me, never yelled at me, and was not a drunk. I never knew the Michael who the police and the newspapers described as a monster."

"What did you tell Michael?"

"I was a broken woman, and I told Michael that I didn't think I had the strength to support him any longer. I had the children to think about, I had bills to pay, and I had my own problems—not least of which was the fact that I had been charged with welfare fraud when I accepted welfare checks for a short period and failed to disclose Michael's true whereabouts. I was afraid such disclosure might lead to Michael being arrested on charges that were still pending in Illinois. I told Michael that I intended to resolve my legal problem and then I was going to pack up and take the children back to Chicago to live with my mother. Our move to Pasco had obviously not worked out, Michael was headed for prison again, this time for a long stretch, and I was ready for the Lord to show me another path."

"So, this was the spring or summer of 1978. You apparently did not leave Pasco and go back to Chicago?" I asked.

"I fully intended to. I started planning to move. I needed to work for a while to save money and I wanted the children to stay in school until I had enough money to buy train tickets and pay off my bills. I also still needed to deal with the welfare fraud charge. Michael had decided to plead guilty to all the charges filed against him in Benton County—you know, the robbery of the Giant T store, the kidnappings, and all that. He was sentenced to several life terms in prison and they sent him off to Walla Walla. I drove from Pasco to Walla Walla to see him on a regular basis, but he knew our relationship was over and that I was taking the children back to Chicago."

"So, what happened to change your mind?"

"It was some strange combination of love, pity, and divine intervention. By the spring of 1979, I had bought train tickets for me and the children. I gave notice that I would be quitting my job and I started packing. Michael was not doing well adjusting to prison life in the penitentiary, but I knew there was nothing I could do about it. I could visit him, give him temporary comfort, but I could no longer live my life for him.

"I was enraged at Michael and grateful, at the same time. My feelings for him were complicated. There is nothing more confusing than being in love with a man who is self-destructive. I was not a weak woman. I was not a victim of domestic violence. My relationship with Michael was soul to soul. I had spent ten years with a man whose life was a disaster and still, when I was with him, felt him, thought about him, it was the inner Michael I experienced. This was the Michael that was unknown to anyone else. It was an act of supreme will for me to make the decision to walk away from him."

Dee paused. I thought she might cry. We were sitting at the dining room table in her nicely furnished, well-ordered Pasco apartment. There were photos of the family everywhere—framed pictures adorned the walls, shelves, and coffee tables. The refrigerator was plastered with prints of the grandchildren and great grandchildren. Michael's face graced several photos that tracked the gradual change in his appearance over the decades. There were snapshots that captured the intense, hard-edged, unsmiling Michael Anderson in his twenties, and others that showed a softer, more genial visage—changes attributable to the pacifying effects of institutionalization and a change in his core being. What I saw in Dee's home was a graphic history of a man who somehow had found a way to connect head and heart and soul.

Dee did not cry. Instead, she got up and walked to a chest of drawers in the living room. She opened a drawer, pulled out a packet of old newspaper clippings, and plopped them down in front of me. They documented Michael Anderson's notorious crimes, some containing photos depicting the supposed beast in prison garb, hunched forward and constrained by chains that tied foot to foot, feet to neck, hand to hand, and hands to feet. Michael's life had led him to this place. He was where society wanted him, bowed and impotent, surrounded by deputies as he shuffled from jail to courtroom and back.

Dee resumed her story. "What happened is simple to explain and maybe hard to understand. We were ready to leave for Chicago. I wanted to see Michael one last time to say goodbye. As it happened, he was now charged with a host of new crimes in Franklin County. It was the spring of 1979. You were representing him, George. He had a hearing scheduled at the courthouse so, rather than driving to the penitentiary to visit him, I thought maybe I could see him briefly at the courthouse before or after his hearing. I walked into the courtroom just before the proceeding began. Michael was

PART 2: DARKNESS

at the lawyer's table with you and Mr. Mahoney. He was hunched over at the waist because of the chains that seemed to be attached to every part of his body. He could barely move. He managed to twist and lift his head just enough to see me. It was the most pathetic thing I had ever seen. I was overwhelmed with emotion. This broken but proud man, the man I had loved for many years, was paraded before the court like a wild animal. I thought of the first time I saw Michael when he was fifteen. He was so strong and confident and attractive. I remembered that at the moment of our first meeting it was revealed to me that Michael and I would spend our lives together. This was not my decision; it was the Lord's.

"When I looked at Michael in that courtroom forty years ago, I knew that the Lord intended me to fulfill that destiny. It was not rational for me to stay with Michael. It made no sense. After all, Michael would spend his life in prison. But, like Abraham, I trusted the Lord and surrendered to his will. It helped that I really did love Michael. Anyway, I stood in that courtroom looking at Michael's hunched back as he faced the court. I did not know how it would all work, but I accepted the reality that I would be there for Michael in whatever way he needed for the rest of my life. I did not know then that this would bring joy to my life as well as pain. I just knew that Michael and I were on the same path. The children and I unpacked our bags, I went back to work, and we stayed in Pasco."

As I listened to Dee talk, I remembered my own feelings as a young lawyer standing in courtrooms with my black client in chains. Were the chains necessary to protect court personnel and law enforcement? Perhaps—Michael had a history of unprovoked violent behavior. Were the chains necessary to guard against escape? Absolutely, Michael was a serial escapee. Still, I objected to the extreme nature of the restraints and the fact my client was paraded around in prison garb surrounded by law enforcement and members of the press. The message projected by the press to the public was antithetical to the law's presumption of innocence. But my gut reaction went deeper. The image of a broken black man in chains encircled by white figures of authority and photographers is an image that leaps out of that lamentable chapter of American history that wounds us to this day.

I asked Dee to talk about her life after she decided to stay in Pasco and remain in a relationship with Michael.

"Michael and I decided to get legally married," she said. "We did so on April 14, 1979, in a ceremony conducted in the penitentiary in Walla Walla by Reverend Zedell Jackson, a wonderful local minister who helped prison inmates and folks in Walla Walla. Conjugal visits started at the prison in 1981. These were called extended family visits. They were a huge development and a real credit to the Department of Corrections's commitment to keeping families together. Washington was one of only a few states in the nation that had such visits at the time. It meant that we could grow as a couple and pray together. It meant Michael could have a relationship with his children, and it restored some small amount of normality to our lives. Initially, the visitation took place in dilapidated old trailers that were moved into the medium-security section of the prison. Later, they provided small apartments surrounded by grass, a basketball court, barbeque grill, and benches. It was on prison grounds, but it felt like we had at least some control and dignity. There is no way our marriage could have survived without these visits.

"In those early years, I did not have a car. I did not even have a driver's license. To see Michael, I would have to pay someone to drive me from Pasco to the prison in Walla Walla. I lived on minimum wage trying to feed and support two children. I hated the fact that this part of the country had no public transportation. It was nothing like what I was used to in Chicago. The fact that I had to pay people to drive me to Walla Walla often meant that we had less food or could not pay bills on time. Even my prison visits created legal problems. I was on probation for welfare fraud and my probation officer forbade me from visiting Michael. When I went to the prison, I used a fake name because I was afraid my probation officer might find out and try to punish me for violating my probation. Later I got a new probation officer, a good guy, who gave me permission to see my husband and the father of my children."

I was interested in the history of conjugal visits in American prisons. It turns out that they were once much more available then they are today. There was nothing conjugal about them when they began in the Mississippi farm labor camps in the early 1900s as an outgrowth of the racist trope that caused administrators to believe black inmates were highly sexual and required sexual intimacy in order to be productive the six out of the seven days a week they were required to work. Mississippi's Parchman Farm had an informal arrangement where sex workers would be driven in by the busload to fraternize with prisoners. This evolved in Mississippi and elsewhere into a legal program for spouses and families to spend time together. The term "conjugal visits" is still a misnomer because "visits" connote visits with close family members, not just spouses. As recently as 1995, nineteen states authorized extended family visits. Today, only four states authorize such visits—Washington, California, New York, and Connecticut. The visits are not allowed at all in the federal prison system.

It seems obvious that extended family visits help sustain families. While physical intimacy is allowed, the visits are not really about sex. They are about creating space and opportunity for families to stay connected and prepare for the eventual release of an offender who hopes someday to return home. The visits also reduce sexual violence in prisons, reduce recidivism, and improve inmate morale and behavior. Nonetheless, several states terminated their programs in the "get tough on crime" era of the last several decades. Legislative and public opinion branded family visits as too generous, too expensive, and too likely to promote smuggling of contraband. There was also negative public sentiment around the possibility that babies might be conceived during these visits. Michael's early life choices made prison inevitable, but at least he wound up in a correctional setting that gave him a chance to keep his family together. It was also a strong incentive for him to avoid conduct that would cause his visits to be forfeited.

I wanted to know about the birth of their third child, nicknamed Babyboy, and how it changed their lives.

"This was God's work," Dee continued. "God gave Michael and me Babyboy as a gift. His birth in 1982 brought us closer together and gave Michael something else to live for. Babyboy was a gift, but his early life was not easy. When he was two, he came down with Kawasaki Disease and almost died. His whole body swelled up, including his head. He was hospitalized at Our Lady of Lourdes Hospital in Pasco for weeks. I could not recognize him when I visited. I would have to prepare myself emotionally just to be in the same room with him. He was on antibiotics and took thirty aspirins a day. He survived, but for the next five years I had to take him to a medical specialist in Spokane for periodic testing. For a while, I was angry with God. But I finally realized that it was God who saved Babyboy, and it was God who made it possible for Michael and me to be this baby's parents. When Babyboy was older, he became very involved in my local church, a Baptist Church, and he turned into a wonderful man. He graduated from high school, went to college, got married, and had his own children. He sells real estate in Las Vegas. The rest is history, a long, unusual, and challenging history, but one filled with love, children, grandchildren, great grandchildren, and a commitment to Christ."

Part 3: (White) Privilege

Chapter 16

"You cannot be afraid to speak up and speak out for what you believe. You have to have courage, raw courage."

—John Lewis

I was raised in southeastern Washington in the embrace of white, middle-class comfort in a big house on a leafy sycamore-lined avenue. The world of my youth was wheat fields and vineyards, swimming, skiing, lemonade stands, and school. What success I have enjoyed in life might have been foretold from foundational elements I took for granted: a supportive family, private school education, travel opportunities, and a moral paradigm constructed from my family's faith tradition and liberalism. I had flirted with drugs and the emerging counterculture of the sixties, but in truth I was a conventional preppie with a contrarian streak.

My mother stayed home to raise my four siblings and me, an undertaking balanced and made tolerable by her civic work, bridge club, charity fundraisers, and church activities. I am pretty good at asking questions, something I learned from watching my mother, who rarely released a stranger from her conversational clutches before extracting the essence of his or her life's story. This would occasionally unnerve the persons interrogated, but more often they would become enduringly enamored of my mom for the simple reason that she made them feel important and valued. Mom's personality could be dominating, sometimes to a fault, but her interest in people, politics, family, and religion was genuine. She adored small talk, so much so that in the evening, and into the wee hours, she was a predictable presence on the living room couch, sipping coffee, maybe a cocktail, waiting and hoping for a family member or friend to wander into her gravitational orbit for a long, meandering exchange. She would usually begin by saying, "Well, now, just tell me everything." If I happened to be the target, I squirmed and connived to escape the interrogation. I wanted privacy and space. Mom's presence was often too weighty and invasive.

The center of my father's universe was his law practice. He, too, liked people, but he was emotionally guarded and less inclined toward small talk. His enthusiasm for life was substantial and may have been even greater and more animated had the war not inflicted some dark and unknowable psychic wound and had the financial demands of a large family and conventions of post-World War II America not enslaved him to his work. He had fought for months on the front lines under General Patton, without a break, from June 7, 1944, the day after D-Day, through the end of Battle of the Bulge in January 1945. Today we know that trauma comes in many forms and has the power to permanently alter how people behave and see the world. Even one day of combat on the front lines during the invasion of Normandy might be enough to cause serious emotional disruption. Multiple months of combat could derail a nervous system for life. Dad never revealed his interior demons, but they were there. He was charming, attractive, and engaging, but in many ways closed off, disconnected, and mercurial. It is hard to imagine him starting a conversation with "Now, just tell me everything."

For different reasons, my parents believed their children should attend traditional boarding schools. Mom was the product of New England Episcopal parents and her sensibility about proper education grew out of the British notion that discipline and the firm hand of a headmaster or headmistress should tame free-spirited children. Dad didn't care about English boarding school traditions, but he did equate private schools with quality education and expanded horizons. My four siblings and I all went to high schools located some distance from Kennewick. They were filled with white kids from affluent homes, some there for academic challenge, some because they needed disciplinary structure, and some because their parents did not want them at home.

At the Episcopal school I attended in Portland, Oregon, none of my peers were poor and there were no black students. Still, for me the overall experience was transformative—an urban environment, stimulating teachers, good friends, athletics, a girlfriend, accountability. I finished high school having developed a real interest in learning and confidence in my ability to face the future.

We took for granted that I would attend college, preferably a reputable college on the East Coast. My father encouraged me to apply to Princeton, my paternal grandfather's college, but I was not admitted. I did get admitted to Bard College—a good liberal arts college on the Hudson River north of Poughkeepsie, New York.

About the same time Michael spent his fifteenth birthday in isolation at the St. Charles School and Home for Boys, I was facing final exams at the end of my freshman year. I had spent the year living the confusion and excitement of early adulthood. I could drink or not, go to class or not, take acid or not, and thereby learn the rewards and challenges of an autonomous life. Society was in turmoil. The Vietnam War and civil rights movement were at a peak. Martin Luther King, Jr. had recently been assassinated. Bobby Kennedy had entered the race for the presidential nomination. *Magical Mystery Tour* songs were being played ubiquitously. After a year adapting to an East Coast culture and hanging out with smart, intense, and assertive students from Boston and New York City, I looked forward to spending the summer under big skies in the relaxed environs of the West.

Just then my eccentric grandfather ("Gramps") unexpectedly showed up in his 1961 Chevy Greenbrier van at my dormitory. Gramps had driven his camper north from Florida where he lived on a retired preacher's budget with my grandmother in a West Palm Beach mobile home park surrounded by mansions and celebrities. He had come north to attend his fiftieth reunion at Trinity College in Connecticut. Gramps was now ready to go home. Tired of driving, and Trinity being in such proximity to Bard, he thought it a good idea to swing by my dorm so I could drive him back to Florida. This was news to me when, returning from an exam, I encountered Gramps waiting for me at my dorm where he had already introduced himself to fellow students and hooked up the Greenbrier's twenty-foot electrical cord.

Gramps—my mother's father—was a retired Episcopal minister possessed of a strong, some would say dominating, personality, unbending opinions, and a large appetite for all manner of worldly indulgences. I remember Gramps pointing to me from the pulpit, as I sat meekly and reluctantly in a large congregation of worshippers at an early Sunday morning service. I was perhaps twelve years old. "Jibber [my family nickname], can you tell us the meaning of today's reading from the Gospel?" Gramps had been a machine gunner in World War I. He was a patriot and an FDR Democrat. Tolerant of other religious traditions, he believed that the gospel of Jesus Christ was instructive in a world that needed more sharing and community. He was no evangelical and operated on the assumption that a life well lived involved lots of baseball and alcohol.

Anyway, I was not too pleased to have this demanding old man walk into my eighteen-year-old life at such an inauspicious time. Gramps said he understood that I had academic obligations and that we would not leave for Florida until my exams were over. In the meantime, he would explore the campus, have a chat with the college president, and contact my professors to see how I was doing. The only thing he required of me was that I be available every evening to join him in the Greenbrier for a meal of boiled meat and potatoes. When I explained that I ate at the college commons with my friends, he assured me that a grateful grandson would happily favor his grandfather with the pleasure of his company at dinner. After a few days, my college friends grew accustomed to this curious old man hanging around the dormitory, and his presence evolved into something of a campus story.

Gramps did talk to the college president, who apparently pretended to know who I was and offered his opinion that I was doing just fine but could work a little harder. We finally left for Florida with me doing most of the driving. I was under strict instructions not to exceed fifty-five miles per hour. Gramps, who spent most of the travel time sleeping in the back of the van, could calculate my speed by the sound of the engine and he would periodically bark at me to slow down. When we got to the Baltimore-Washington, DC metropolitan area, I turned the wheel over to Gramps so I could sleep for a bit. I emphasized how important it was to stay on the freeway that skirted the cities, but Gramps called to me sometime later saying he was a "little lost." I woke up to find we were smack in the middle of downtown Baltimore, skyscrapers on both sides, and Gramps accusing me of not having plotted a better route.

We drove to Selma, Alabama, where we were scheduled to meet my sister Ann, who was a VISTA volunteer working with the rural black community in the small village of Annemanie outside of Selma. The plan was to meet Ann at a local Holiday Inn restaurant to spend some time together before Gramps and I moved on to our destination in Florida. Ann brought with her a lovely young female friend, a black woman from Annemanie. No problem, right? The civil rights movement had sensitized Americans to the importance of equal rights. *Brown v. Board of Education* had been on the books for almost fifteen years and the Civil Rights Act prohibiting discrimination in public accommodations had been enacted four years previously. But this was Selma, the Selma of police dog and water hose fame.

The young white waitress, no doubt operating under the watchful eye of an older manager, refused to acknowledge our presence among the handful of white customers. Gramps instructed us to stay put, as he walked across the street to purchase a six-pack of beer and some soda pop at a local market. He returned, opened a beer can, and proceeded to drink and talk loudly about the shame of Southern racism. My sister implored him to simply leave, arguing that we could find another place—a black establishment—where we would be welcome. But Gramps was unyielding, drinking beer after beer and talking even more provocatively, as he became increasingly inebriated. I sipped my soda and waited to be beaten up or arrested. In time, the manager asked us to leave, and Gramps responded that we would—after we had ordered and eaten. We continued to be ignored but not assaulted or imprisoned. We eventually left the restaurant and said goodbye to my sister, her friend, and this toxic town that symbolized the piece of America that could not reconcile its affection for the rhetoric of freedom with the right of a young black women to order a simple meal in a public place.

For me, this was not just an anxious encounter with the vestiges of Jim Crow; it was a game changer in terms of how I viewed Gramps. He became more than a colorful and domineering old man—he had morphed into a complex and admirable person of courage and conviction. We finished our trip to Florida, and I went on with my life. Perhaps Gramps had unnecessarily put us at risk but, in my memory, he will always be the guy who steadfastly drank a six-pack and railed against racism at a time and place when most folks would have chosen discretion over valor.

Chapter 17

*"Just remember two things. First, help people whenever possible.
Second, avoid hurting people whenever possible."*

—Nez Perce Elder

I spent one year at Bard before dropping out on the hunch that what was happening in the streets of America in 1968 was more interesting than what was happening in the classroom. I wanted to experience it all—war protest, the civil rights movement, generational rebellion, drugs, sex, and rock and roll.

So, while Michael Anderson was dating Dee in Illinois, I wandered the West Coast and spent time in San Francisco, Berkeley, Eugene, and Seattle. I enrolled in different colleges, dropped out when school was inconvenient, skied in the winter, worked menial jobs when my father tired of supporting my lifestyle, and generally immersed myself in the freedom and culture of the late sixties and seventies. In time, I collected enough credits to obtain a bachelor's degree in English Literature. I graduated from the University of Washington in 1972. These were good years and they were unburdened by many of the challenges and concerns faced by young people today. I was excited to be alive and I valued the emergence of the youth culture. My college debt was minimal, and I did not worry about the earth becoming uninhabitable. There was, however, a specter that haunted the entire nation, especially draft-eligible males: Vietnam.

While I followed sports, I was not much interested in boxing, which always struck me as unnecessarily brutal and atavistic. It was therefore unexpected that Muhammad Ali would become my hero and a powerful role model whose strength of character and conviction illuminated much about the clash of values and choices that marked the sixties and seventies. At a time when I was drafted and had to decide about going to war or not, Ali showed the way. He gave up his crown, millions of dollars, and suffered public obloquy to face jail for his refusal to join the army. Unschooled in grammar and unflinching in honesty and resolve, he framed an anti-war and anti-draft argument persuasively and eloquently in the language of conscience and human rights:

> My conscience won't let me go shoot my brother, or some poor hungry people in the mud for big powerful America. And shoot them for what? They never called me nigger, they never lynched me, they didn't put no dogs on me, they didn't rob me of my nationality, rape and kill my mother and father. Shoot them for what? How can I shoot them poor people? Just take me to jail.

The war was fought largely by poor people of color and poor white kids who were either true believers, indifferent, or unschooled in draft evasion strategies. To create a more predictable flow of recruits, and to spread the pain more equitably, the federal government implemented the first draft lottery in history, a lottery that randomly assigned a number to 365 possible birthdays. The lower your number, the more likely you would get drafted. There would be no more student deferments.

On that December day in 1969, a few weeks before Christmas, friends and I gathered around a cramped student apartment in Seattle's university district to listen to the methodical process of picking numbers that would send some to war and allow others to continue down a less anxious path. It had been announced in advance that those with birthdays correlating to the numbers 1 through 140 would likely be drafted. I was attending the University of Washington, studying Shakespeare and the English Romantic poets, and dating Francie, a spunky, smart, and pretty young woman who had recently transferred to UW from the University of Pennsylvania, and who was serendipitously from Kennewick— my hometown. By 1969, I was a committed and passionate opponent of the Vietnam War. I took no pleasure in having my birthday entered in a drawing that would determine who might kill or be killed. We did not breathe as the radio announcer proclaimed each successive number. He got through number eighty and I was safe. Not for long. My birthday, April 4, was picked next and I knew my life would change.

I did get drafted and appeared for the required army physical in Spokane. After I was determined to be sufficiently fit physically and morally to kill peasants 10,000 miles away, I submitted a petition to be classified as a conscientious objector based on my opposition to war that derived from my belief in a transcendent power. My draft board in conservative Pasco, Washington had not granted a CO petition since the Korean War. That fact did not inspire confidence; nor did the fact that I had cited an unspecified "transcendent power" instead of "the Father, the son, and the Holy Spirit," the more traditional Christian and Trinitarian formulation of divinity that, to my way of thinking, was far more mysterious then my straightforward allusion to the transcendent.

To support my petition, I secured letters from prep school teachers, college professors, Episcopal clergy, lawyers, judges, and friends. Some months later, shortly before Muhammad Ali won his conscientious objector appeal to the Supreme Court, I received a letter saying my petition was granted, subject to my obligation to perform two years of alternative public service in an approved civilian capacity. I was happy to do so, and I fulfilled my obligation as a VISTA volunteer working for a rural, low-income housing project in central California following my college graduation.

My resistance to the war was honest and principled, and I was relieved to finally get the Vietnam monkey off my back. However, I was haunted then, and I am haunted now, by knowledge that I got a CO classification because of privilege. Regardless of how strong another young man's commitment to the transcendent might have been, if he had been an unconnected, poorly educated, impoverished young African American or Native American, it is unlikely he could have marshalled the know-how and resources that enabled me to avoid going to war.

* * * *

The 1970s—what a decade for youth and freedom! Some say it was really still the sixties and there is great truth in that, insofar as I remember. But the sixties was also a time of great anxiety—at least for me, and perhaps for most people of my generation. We were kids, many of us spoiled, and we could not really be sure what would happen when we were someday made to be adults. So, there was a sense, at least a suspicion, that all of it might not survive—the energy, the buzz, the drugs, the music, the manifold reimagining of the culture, of mind, body and spirit, of the earth, of an egalitarian world; that adulthood and responsibility could turn us into our parents or worse, a fractured generation, privileged by a glimpse of what might be, but trapped in a world of what has been.

The 1970s, though, presented a cultural menu that permitted one to taste all that the '60s had to offer: the music, the drugs, the anti-war passion, meditation, civil rights, cinema, environmental science, feminist theory, and sex—all of it without the anxiety of endless war, uncertain futures, disappointed parents, legal segregation, Richard Nixon (after 1974), broken-down cars, and no college degree. At some point in the seventies, the children of the sixties had a grip on the future, some with college degrees, some with jobs, some with spouses and children. They were still feeling loose and flexible, but not necessarily lost. Their parents were not yet sick or feeble, and they did not yet have to shoulder the burdens that come with running the world.

Following my civilian service as a conscientious objector, I spent the summer of 1974 among free spirits in the mountain resort town of McCall, Idaho. These folks were back-to-the-land granola types, cafeteria hippies, part-time students, and true spiritual explorers. Some were simply homeless wanderers. What they had in common was an affection for getting high. McCall was situated on Payette Lake, north of Boise and not far south of where the Little Salmon River converges with the Lower Salmon at the town of Riggins. Historically, the area was a perennial summer gathering place for the Nez Perce and Shoshone Indian tribes. The twentieth century had brought gold prospectors, loggers, tourism, and hippies.

The summer was a long party, and I regretted leaving to start law school at Gonzaga University in Spokane. I had reservations about going to law school. My main concern was not that my party days were over but fear that law school would throw my life out of balance, bury me in mind-numbing minutiae, and rob me of passion and authenticity. My father had a successful and rewarding law practice, but he also suffered from work addiction and stress associated with having to meet the financial demands of a busy law office and a large family. I knew that law school was a path to a fulfilling and meaningful career—an opportunity to make a difference in the world—but I wondered if it was possible to be a lawyer while remaining faithful to my maverick nature.

Filled with anxiety and anticipation, I climbed into my aging and iconic black Volvo—the snail-like model with the rounded back and protruding front end—in late summer and left McCall for Spokane. I followed Highway 95 as it snaked north along the bluffs above the Salmon River, south of White Bird, Idaho. My leisurely drive was abruptly interrupted by screeching metal coming from below and behind. The Volvo shuddered and dropped its drive train, differential, and rear axle along several hundred feet of asphalt. I coasted to the shoulder and sat for a long stretch brooding about the meaning of this random and inauspicious event. I finally stepped out of my wounded black snail to survey the damage. Pieces of metal, car

PART 3: (WHITE) PRIVILEGE

parts, things necessary for engines to transfer power to wheels, were scattered everywhere. I was in the middle of nowhere in the Idaho Panhandle. Was this just a chance encounter with the law of entropy, or an omen telling me I should not go to law school?

I walked a bit until I came to a spot on a bluff overlooking a quiet sandy beach on a beautiful bend of the Lower Salmon River as it came out of the mountains from the east and carved a path to the Snake River below Hells Canyon. The bluff protected a sandy beach and overlooked rapids and a vista that faded to the south and west along the distant peaks of the Wallowa Mountains, the traditional homeland of Chief Joseph and his Nez Perce band, a place to which they never returned following their internment on remote reservation lands. It was early afternoon. The sun broke through massive cumulus clouds that streaked upwards to form thunderheads threatening rain to the south. Bits of sunlight escaped the clouds and touched the tops of quaking aspens and cottonwoods perched along the river beneath evergreens that reigned in the high country above.

Then I saw a makeshift hut on the beach below and an old man cooking over an open pit fire. I scrambled down the bluff and introduced myself. He was a Nez Perce Indian, and he was cooking freshly caught trout, which he offered to me without hesitation. He didn't talk much. I inquired about the fishing, and he said the river had always provided for him. We sat in silence. I nibbled on the trout and wrestled about what to do—now and tomorrow and for the rest of my life. We smoked cigarettes and looked out across the river and mountains into the late afternoon sun. Finally, he turned to me and said: "You seem anxious."

I told him about the demise of my beloved Volvo.

He said, "But that's just a car. Something else is bothering you."

I poured out my story to this stranger, as though confessing to a priest. I told him of my father's life, my decision to go to law school, my anxiety, my fear that I could not be a lawyer and still be the person I wanted to be.

He was quiet for awhile, and then he said, "You will be fine. Just remember two things. First, help people whenever possible. Second, avoid hurting people whenever possible. Don't worry about the car. There are lots of cars."

I climbed the bluff back up to the highway and stuck out my thumb. A guy who loved old Volvos picked me up, offered me a toke of some powerful weed, gave me $300 for my Volvo, and took me to the next town. From there I made my way to Spokane, to a life in the law and beyond.

Part 4: Due Process and Equal Protection

Chapter 18

*"In all criminal prosecutions, the accused shall enjoy the right
... to have the Assistance of Counsel for his defense."*

—Sixth Amendment, US Constitution

Michael Anderson and I both came to southwestern Washington at the same time, toward the end of 1977, about the time John Travolta ruled the dance floor in *Saturday Night Fever*. Michael came to escape his demons. I was there to practice law, especially criminal law. As it turned out, Michael's demons were powerful, causing his criminal proclivities and my professional interests to intersect in 1979. We spent many days together that year in courtrooms from Spokane to Pasco.

Judge Albert Yencopal was a committed Catholic and a good man. His immigrant Czechoslovakian family had come to Washington at the turn of the century and worked the silver mines in the northern Cascade Mountains. He served in the Pacific during World War II and then went to law school at Gonzaga in Spokane. My dad had also gone to Gonzaga and was a close friend. Dad helped Yencopal become a municipal judge in Richland in 1965 and later supported him when he was elected to the bi-county Benton-Franklin County Superior Court in 1972.

The judge was known for creative and compassionate sentencing in criminal cases, and defense lawyers with a sympathetic client or a compelling story hoped he might be assigned to their case. Prosecutors viewed him as a bleeding heart, no more so than on the occasion when he ignored the prosecutor's recommendation of a life sentence and, instead, gave a young mother who killed her two infant children a sentence of probation and psychiatric treatment. Everyone who followed the case knew the woman with no criminal history was nuts when, in response to God's mandate, she threw her kids off the Kennewick-Pasco bridge and thereby saved their souls from eternal damnation. The jury did not buy her insanity defense, but Yencopal understood that a life sentence at taxpayers' expense would serve no purpose.

On a Friday morning in April 1979, I was in the small town of Prosser handling routine legal matters at the Benton County Courthouse when Judge Yencopal invited me into his chambers for a cup of coffee. He was an unassuming man of few words. There was nothing intimidating about him except, at times, his cryptic manner of expression. His angular facial features were softened by his small frame, ample belly, and humble disposition. He was not an intellectual, not like the other judges who felt compelled to proclaim at length so people might know the discerning analysis that led to their ruling on this or that pedestrian issue. Judge Yencopal let his decisions speak for themselves. I did not expect to have a deep conversation about law, policy, or politics.

He began, "George, we need to appoint someone on a criminal case in Franklin County. There are several counts and the case will involve a little work, but I think you can handle it."

"Great," I replied. "What are the charges?" The judge knew I was just recently out of law school and had joined my father's law firm. He also knew I was interested in criminal trial work. I guessed he wanted to throw me some routine business that might advance my professional development while discharging the court's obligation to provide counsel to an indigent defendant.

The judge sipped his coffee and appeared to casually review the documents contained in a file on his desk. "Well, it's sort of an interesting case. There has been a bit of publicity. Perhaps you've seen it. Defendant's name is Michael Anderson, and he's facing a bunch of charges, you know—escape, kidnapping, assault, rape, robbery . . ."

I gulped and immediately thought I had gotten it wrong. The judge must have been talking to me as a representative of my father's law firm with the intention that I would communicate to my father the court's desire to appoint him on the Anderson case.

"You mean you would like to appoint my dad, Judge?"

"No, I mean I want to appoint you." Judge Yencopal looked at me over the reading glasses balanced at the tip of his long Slavic nose.

I quickly composed myself, not wanting to appear too overwhelmed or insecure. Of course, I knew all about Anderson, was aware that he had already pled guilty to several charges in Benton County and was likely going to spend a long stretch in the state penitentiary. Maybe the court figured it didn't matter who represented him on the Franklin County charges because his goose was already cooked. Or maybe the court hoped to save the county money by appointing a young attorney who would not overwork the case and who would not seek the sizeable fees commanded by an older and more experienced lawyer. I was caught between feelings of being flattered and a suspicion that the court was trying to get the Anderson case handled as expeditiously and cheaply as possible.

"Judge, I'm flattered you would consider me competent to handle a matter as substantial as this. I'm familiar with the case from the press reports. I'd like to look at the pleadings before agreeing to the appointment, but I can tell you right now that if you want me to handle it, I'm going to need some help."

"I agree. The case could use a couple of lawyers. Let me know who you want to work with, and I'll arrange for appointment of co-counsel."

His eyes returned to the papers spread across his desk, and I sensed the meeting was over. I rose to exit the judge's chambers.

As I opened the door, Judge Yencopal looked up. "George, I know you will give this man good and competent representation. He will get a fair shake with you at his side. And I suppose I don't need to tell you—if you have any questions, just ask your old man."

My head was spinning as I drove the thirty miles through sagebrush and farmland back to my office in Richland. I tried to organize and address the questions and concerns that besieged me as I considered Judge Yencopal's request. Should I even accept the appointment? Was I a wimp if I didn't? Is it ever good form to turn down a judge? If I did take the case, who should I recommend as co-counsel? How would I handle the challenges presented by the high-profile nature of the case? How much work would be involved? How much would the county compensate me? Would the appointment interfere with my ability to serve my other clients?

The one thing that did not worry me was figuring out legal angles and strategies. I was still at an early stage in my career, but I knew that competent legal work was a function of two things: hard work and caring.

There was one question that weighed on me most. Who was this man, Michael Anderson, and how would we relate to one another?

Critchlow teaching Human Rights Law to Saudi Arabian students in Riyadh; with his daughter on the Queen Elizabeth II sailing for England.

On the Inca Trail to Machu Picchu; and with his wife in the early 1990s before they were married.

Marching for human rights in Spokane with his family and friends.

Baby Michael; as a teenager (right) at the St. Charles Boys Home in Illinois.

Buff and dangerous in the Washington State Penitentiary; with his mother following his commitment to Jesus.

Grandfather Michael

Chapter 19

"Lawyers are people too, some of them..."
—Dick Cavett

A long week was ending, and I would spend the weekend looking at court files and newspaper reports relating to Michael Anderson. I called Tim Mahoney and invited him to stop by my office for a drink after work. He liked stopping by the office, my dad's office, the home of the Critchlow and Williams law firm, housed in a nicely furnished rectangular brick building that featured an interior courtyard and fountain. The Jadwin Avenue address was a desirable location on a block full of similar buildings, all examples of post-war modernism designed to project comfort and simplicity without undue ornamentation.

Critchlow and Williams was formed in the 1950s by my father and David Williams, two progressive lawyers in a hidebound community. Over time, the firm grew, adding partners and associates, all of whom were trial lawyers. The firm specialized in plaintiff's personal injury work, labor law, family law, criminal defense, social security, employment, and civil rights law. It generally represented working people rather than major businesses and insurance companies. The law firm was traditional in appearance, but it was known to advocate for unpopular causes and clients, including the folks I represented in the early years of my law career.

The office had a special room that doubled as a law library and bar. It was the law firm's gravitational center when a lawyer desired to escape telephones and people to research and ponder the law in a quiet, undisturbed setting. In the late afternoon and early evening, it was a place to kick back.

The room was adorned with drawings depicting lawyers and judges in poses and settings ranging from the flattering to the untoward. There was a TV and a huge oak table—round, democratic, and ample enough to accommodate many of King Arthur's knights. Files, trial exhibits, and yellow legal pads littered the room. Law books—the state code, state and federal reporters, legal encyclopedias, and specialty books—covered the table until and unless one of the more fastidious lawyers or legal assistants could no longer tolerate the disorder. There were no computers.

Leather-bound law books were shelved in a series of antique oak bookcases with sliding glass windows, bookcases bequeathed to my dad from his father, a Salt Lake City lawyer named George Critchlow and, later, from my father to me. They lined the room and intimated the presence of a cryptic body of knowledge and wisdom accessible only to members of the bar—the elite folks described by Tocqueville as America's aristocracy.

By late afternoon on any given day, Tocqueville's aristocrats became common people whose stressful lives drove them to venues where their disappointments and successes might be soothed or celebrated with a good whiskey or a dependable bottle of blue-collar beer. The preferred afternoon venue for members of my father's firm was the firm library. Around five or six o'clock, the subdued research and study space morphed effortlessly into a gathering place for cocktails, legal tales, political commentary, bar and judicial gossip, and sports talk.

Tim Mahoney loved the after-hours ambience of the Critchlow and Williams library and readily accepted my invitation to join me for a beer after work. Tim was a young lawyer who was building a general practice in Kennewick, his hometown. I knew Tim well because we were housemates for a while in law school. He graduated a few years before me, but we picked up the relationship again when I went to work for my dad in Richland, just seven miles from Kennewick. Tim was not afraid of the courtroom, and he had the equilibrium and good sense one might expect of the eldest son of a big Irish Catholic family. I liked and respected both those attributes, but there was something else I was looking for if I was going to take on the defense of a man charged with twenty-two felonies, any one of which could keep him in prison for life.

I knew this was not a case that would come down to clever jury arguments or polished courtroom histrionics. Anderson was a convicted felon doing serious time. He was a black man in a county where the jury was likely to be white, some of them bigoted. He was, in fact, a convicted felon who had confessed to many of the criminal acts with which he was currently charged. While I had not yet received or read the voluminous police reports, witness statements, and laboratory reports, and even though I had at that point tried only a handful of jury trials, I suspected the case would involve three goals: obtaining as impartial a jury as possible, excluding inadmissible prejudicial evidence, and reducing the charges to a lesser

PART 4: DUE PROCESS AND EQUAL PROTECTION

degree. Regardless of the issues, I knew that criminal jury trials, from the defense side, required hard work, creative thinking, and belief in the principle that prosecutions should not be based on evidence that was illegally seized, tainted, manufactured, or otherwise unreliable.

Mahoney liked two things. He liked to work hard, and he liked to play basketball. There wasn't much else. I wanted Tim to be my co-counsel on the Anderson case because he was not easily intimidated and because of his work ethic. He also had common sense, an attribute that might be a useful counterweight to my tendency to lose myself in abstraction and idealism while forgetting pedestrian matters like budgets and the tendency of judges to favor their own re-election over unpopular judicial decisions. I knew if we put our minds together and worked hard we could give Anderson the kind of defense that converted the rhetoric of due process and equal justice into something meaningful and real. Or maybe I was engaging in magical thinking. What does a meaningful and real defense mean for a client who was already in prison for life?

It was six in the evening when Tim walked into the library eager to unload the considerable weight of his opinion about a judge who recently denied a motion Tim believed to be a slam dunk. I offered him a beer and listened. Unlike some lawyers, Tim did not believe his cases and clients to be the center of the legal universe. His war stories were communicated humorously, succinctly, and in a manner that was proportionate to the importance of the subject matter. He finished venting, sipped his beer, and probed. "So, what's up? The old man working your ass off?"

"Well, he sure has me getting up earlier than I like," I answered. "I can't really complain because he still gets to work earlier than I do, has a million clients, and makes more money talking to an insurance adjuster for fifteen minutes than I can make in a month."

"Anything interesting?"

"Well, yes, possibly. That's the reason I asked you to stop by—Michael Anderson, as in the Michael Anderson who has been all over the news the last year. Yencopal wants to appoint me on the Franklin County charges, all twenty-two—robberies, kidnapping, assaults, who knows what else."

Tim's head tilted back slightly, and his eyes widened.

"Wow, George. He's a real badass. The press will be all over it. People will hate you. I'm not sure Yencopal's doing you a favor. There's no way Anderson could possibly get a fair trial—at least not around here. I mean it's hard enough for a black guy to get a break even if he wasn't a convicted felon."

"Yeah, well, you know . . . someone has to represent him," I offered. "People are going to hate us lawyers anyway . . . until they get busted, ripped off, or need a divorce."

"I'm a little surprised they're going after him on more charges. Isn't he already doing several life sentences on the Benton County charges? Judge Frederick hated him. I remember reading something about Frederick saying Anderson should never be paroled."

"I'm betting they're pursuing the Franklin County charges to reinforce that message to the parole board," I suggested. "Seems everyone wants him to die in prison."

"Yeah, but it's not like he murdered someone," Tim pointed out. "And it's going to cost them a ton of money. They'll probably have to change venue, pay you, pay for experts. I don't know, seems kinda pointless if he's already going to spend most of his life in prison."

"Could be partly political," I replied. "The Franklin County prosecutor is up for re-election next year. He could score some points with the case. I mean, consider the scenario—convicted felon escapes from jail, invades home, assaults family with a gun, beats and kidnaps mom, puts her in a trunk, takes her as a hostage to Seattle. Pretty provocative stuff. Add the fact that he's black, and you have a lot of enraged voters."

Tim came back to the point about distinguishing murder, the ultimate crime, from lesser crimes. "There are murderers who get paroled. Anderson didn't kill anyone."

"True, but the system doesn't favor black convicted felons who terrorize white communities," I countered.

Tim nodded and lifted his beer. He stared at the label and then took a long swig. He addressed the obvious question.

"No offense, but I would have expected them to appoint someone who's a bit more experienced. I wonder what's up."

"Me too," I answered. I had been consumed by the question since my conversation with Judge Yencopal. "I was thinking maybe they hope to get this done on the cheap, that I won't put up much of a fight, maybe get him to plead like he did on the Benton County charges. You know . . . give the guy a lawyer because the Constitution requires it, but make sure it's not Gerry Spence or my dad. Appoint a newbie who wants to make a quick buck and get his name in the paper but won't raise too much of a fuss."

Tim picked up the thread. "In other words, find a young lawyer who sees this as a mere formality—a necessary process—but not one that is going to matter much since the defendant is going to spend most of his life in prison no matter what happens."

"Exactly. But, you know, Tim, I don't really think that's what's going on. First, why the hell would Yencopal think that I would be that kind of lawyer? Why would he appoint someone from the Critchlow and Williams law firm, a firm he knows is a strong advocate for equal rights? Why would he pick the son of a good friend? I think Yencopal appointed me because he would like Anderson to get a serious, bona fide defense. He knows these other judges and the Franklin County prosecutor are going to be tough on this guy, and I believe Yencopal wants him to get a fair shake."

Tim nodded. "Plus, the judge knows by appointing you he gets the benefit of your dad's assistance without having to pay for it. Still, even though you can brainstorm with your dad, you are going to have to do all the heavy lifting by yourself. And take all the heat."

"Not necessarily. I told Yencopal I would need some help, and he agreed. He told me he would appoint co-counsel. I want you to be my co-counsel." I raised my beer to salute our proposed partnership.

Tim grimaced for a moment and then grinned. "That's a hell of a lot of work, George. Lots of press, challenging issues, a despised client, hostile jurors, crochety judges, low pay. Sounds fun. When do we start? And, seriously, how much are we going to get paid?"

"We start tomorrow. And I'm sure the pay will be lousy."

"Okay, but just remember, I play basketball on Saturday mornings."

Chapter 20

> "... nor shall any State deprive any person of life, liberty, or property, without due process of law; nor deny to any person within its jurisdiction the equal protection of the laws."
>
> —Fourteenth Amendment, US Constitution

From the beginning of the case, Tim and I considered it obvious that our client should not and could not be tried in Franklin County. The prospect for assembling an impartial, untainted jury was zero. Anderson's name, face, and history had been plastered on pages of the newspaper and recycled on repeated television news broadcasts over several months. He was widely known as a convicted felon from Chicago who now resided in the state penitentiary because of pleading guilty to various crimes in Benton County. The family he was accused of terrorizing in Franklin County was a respected salt-of the-earth Pasco clan whose kinship with the community ran deep. People who knew nothing about the case would have difficulty keeping their minds open, much less those who already reviled Anderson and looked forward to his eternal damnation. Every criminal defense lawyer knows it is one thing to talk about impartial justice and the presumption of innocence; it is another thing to achieve it in practice.

There was another factor that convinced me the case should not be tried in Pasco. Race. African American people lived in Pasco, yes, but they rarely showed up on jury panels. And the people who did serve on juries were frequently the kind of community-minded Caucasians who took pride in knowing what was best for black folks. Some might interpret this last comment as nothing more than an expression of hypercritical liberal bias, but I was not a newcomer to the area, and I knew something about the predilection of Franklin County jurors. In fact, the lesson I had learned about Franklin County jurors was fresh in mind from a recent case I had tried in that venue.

PART 4: DUE PROCESS AND EQUAL PROTECTION

* * * *

Sam and Dorothy were born, raised and married—to one another—in early twentieth-century Mississippi. Like many African Americans, including Michael Anderson's ancestors, they lived in rural poverty with little chance of rising above the station assigned by history and culture to poor and poorly educated southern blacks. They decided to join the migration out of the South to northern venues they believed would provide economic opportunity and an escape from pervasive discrimination. Sam heard there were good railroad jobs in the Northwest, so he brought Dorothy to Pasco just after serving with the US Army in the European theater during World War II. Sam worked as a laborer in the old railroad roundhouse that repositioned locomotives back when Pasco was an important railroad hub. The job was steady, and it supported the couple's growing family.

Living in Pasco offered more opportunity than Mississippi, but postwar Pasco for African Americans was not a Norman Rockwell picture of the American dream. Pasco was a segregated town where custom and practice consigned blacks to live in several blocks of low-income rentals and modest homes on the city's east side. The remainder of the city was predominately white. So was the county, a big county with miles of open, undeveloped land mixed in with large wheat, grass, and potato farms.

When I was young, there were no blacks in Kennewick, just a half-mile across the river from Pasco. That situation was preserved by informal custom rather than official Jim Crow laws. This was the north where blacks learned where they could reside by trial and error, and by the largesse or exclusivity of those white people who controlled lending, real estate, and local government.

As it happened, Sam and Dorothy were renters. They were never able to afford their own home during Sam's working years. But, since coming north, the couple dreamed of buying and owning their own place. So, for decades they had set a little money aside each month to make their goal a reality. It was not until the kids had grown and Sam was retired from his railroad job that the couple finally felt they had saved enough to start shopping for a home they could call their own. They had noticed that a huge parcel of land had recently been developed in Pasco for manufactured homes. The development was complete with curbs, gutters, electricity, sewer and water. The project consisted of dozens of vacant lots. It was located just north of East Pasco's historical black district. A major sales effort was underway, but no one had yet moved a manufactured home onto a site. The year was 1976.

The couple did their research and decided to put money down on a manufactured home that would be delivered to them once they had purchased a suitable lot. They knew the lot they wanted. It was situated on the northwest corner of the new development with a view into Pasco to the west and open county land to the north. The parcel was not far, perhaps a half mile, from the neighborhood in which they had lived for years as renters. They approached the development's marketing office and communicated their interest in buying the lot on the northwest corner. The white sales employee politely informed them that, unfortunately, that lot had already been promised to someone else. Sam and Dorothy recovered from their disappointment and quickly decided on an alternative lot. They were surprised to find that that lot had also been sold. They thought it odd there was no public sign or other indication these two lots were unavailable. Not to worry, there were plenty of other newly developed lots that went on for blocks. They expressed interest in still another lot only to be told there was a problem with that lot's utility hook-ups, and the lot was not currently for sale. When they inquired about still another lot, and another, they were given varying explanations as to why the lots could not be sold.

Sam and Dorothy did not have the privilege of extensive schooling, but they knew a few things about how the world worked. They knew the official recipe for achieving the American dream: work hard, take care of your family, serve your country, and have faith in God. They had done it all. They were humble, God-fearing people who had raised a family, worked hard, and fought for freedom. Sam and Dorothy also knew the alternative narrative, the lived narrative of people of color who learn from experience that no matter what kind of lives they live, some doors will be closed. The couple politely told the sales agent that they believed the development was not open to black people. The salesman expressed shock and assured them that if they came back—perhaps in a few months—he was sure he could find them a suitable lot.

Sam and Dorothy did not return to the sales office. They went, instead, to see a lawyer—my father. He quickly filed a discrimination lawsuit in the Franklin County Superior Court, alleging violations of the couples' state and federal civil rights. It was about this time that I went to work for my dad. Knowing of my interest in civil rights, he gave the case to me and remarked that it might not be worth a lot of money, but it was among the most important cases in the office. He also mentioned that Sam and Dorothy were about the nicest people you would ever want to meet.

I pulled up to the modest, wood-framed home in the center of East Pasco's black community. The street was littered with junk vehicles. Lawns were brown and dry. Most structures needed paint. I wanted to see Sam and Dorothy's aging rental house and have them show me the development where they had hoped to live in their new manufactured home. They met me at the door and ushered me into a clean and tidy, nicely furnished living room adorned with pictures of Martin Luther King, John Kennedy, and Pope Paul VI. There were more pictures of their two boys, now grown and on their own. Sam was tall, slender, and taciturn. His wife was diminutive and effusive.

They offered me coffee, and we chatted about their early lives in Mississippi, their move to the Northwest, and their efforts to create a secure and stable family life. Dorothy related that the neighborhood had once been family friendly but in recent years had gone downhill. There were drugs and crime. I asked what home ownership meant for them, and they responded with what any American might say, regardless of race or station. Home ownership represented safety and security, independence, and a means for getting ahead financially. People take pride in home ownership, and it symbolizes achievement. Sam and Dorothy had talked about these things for years.

The trial took place after months of pretrial skirmishing aimed at discovering documents and communications that might disclose and prove the discriminatory intentions of the defendant corporation that refused to sell to my clients. Depositions and informal interviews with witnesses had shown what I believed was a shared understanding among corporate officers and employees that they would not let black people buy into the development for fear that it would gain a reputation as a "black development." No one would admit this squarely, but several people opined that black folks would have no problem buying lots once the majority of lots were sold first to white buyers. I also discovered there was no impediment to selling my clients any of the lots in which they had expressed interest. They had been lied to. By the time of trial, white people had purchased these lots.

We selected an all-white Franklin County jury. I had hoped against all odds that there might be one or two African Americans selected, but the jury panel called by the court was overwhelmingly white. The one black citizen called to come forward during the selection process was promptly "struck" by the defendant's attorney who, at that time, had the legal right to use what are called "peremptory challenges" to remove up to three prospective jurors without stating a reason. The jurors we ended up with were local people, most of them raised in Pasco, the town that had been dubbed the "Birmingham of the Northwest" during the civil rights struggles of the 1960s.

I was pleased with how things went, especially since it was one of my first civil jury trials. I worked my butt off and was successful in getting my witnesses to say what I hoped they would say. On cross-examination, I hammered adverse witnesses who I knew to be lying. It was a good sign when the defendant's lawyer finally offered to settle the case for several thousand dollars during trial. By that time, we had considerable expenses invested in the case; my clients had lost their down payment on the manufactured home, and we were convinced the evidence would support a substantial award of both compensatory and punitive damages. My only reservation stemmed from the fact that the jurors seemed uncomfortable and refused to look me in the eye. In any event, my clients rejected the settlement offer, and the trial concluded with a rousing closing argument that I had waited my whole life to give.

We had been in trial for eight days. The jury deliberated for two days. This was good because I assumed the long deliberation meant jurors were arguing over how substantial the award of damages should be. Finally, the jury reassembled in the courtroom. We waited anxiously and heard the foreman announce the jury's answer to the court's first question: Did the defendant corporation discriminate against Sam and Dorothy based on race—yes or no? The foreman answered, "Yes." My heart leaped—we won! The foreman went on to answer the second question: "If the answer to the first question is "yes," what are plaintiffs' damages? The foreman lowered his eyes and mumbled the jury's answer: "Zero."

I was devastated. The clients were more philosophical. They took the verdict in stride, as they had learned to take things in stride their entire lives. I asked the court's permission to interview individual jurors, at least those willing to talk with me. Two jurors shared with me how their deliberations led to a verdict of discrimination, but no damage. The explanation went something like this: "Well, yes, the developer did discriminate, you proved that. But you should remember, this is Pasco, and we just felt that your clients were better off and happier living with their own kind rather than forcing themselves into a community that did not want them. So, since your clients were better off, not worse off, we just didn't see any damage."

This statement of the jurors' sense of justice may be the most succinct and forthright declaration of white privilege and racial paternalism I have ever heard. The trial court refused my request for a new trial. The judge considered the verdict to be a judgment for the defendant. I appealed. A year later the court of appeals reversed the trial court in a written decision that affirmed the legal principle that a verdict of discrimination automatically mandated an award of at least nominal damages and attorney's fees. The appellate court assessed damages in the amount of $100 and sent the case back to the trial judge to calculate legal fees. In the end, the defendant paid my dad's law firm several thousand dollars in legal fees and $100 to Sam and Dorothy. My dad instructed me to send the legal fees to our clients. The incongruity of the outcome was just too much for him.

Chapter 21

"We will only begin to forgive when we can look upon the wrongdoers as ourselves, neither better nor worse. We need to remember that we coexist as mortals in the world, together, the wronged and the wrongdoer, and that, in our common humanity, the situation could readily be reversed."

—Leo Buscaglia

Before Tim and I read the police reports, reviewed the evidence, or analyzed the legal elements of the charges, indeed, before we had even met our client, we decided to prepare a motion asking the court to change the venue of *State of Washington v. Michael Anderson* to another county, preferably a distant, multiracial county with judges and jurors who had never heard of Michael Anderson. We were not only interested in getting away from local jurors; we wanted to avoid local judges who had already sentenced Anderson in other prosecutions, who were steeped in the case, and who would at some point have to face unforgiving voters whose racial attitudes might be less than charitable and whose negative view of our client was permanently imprinted.

Another matter, a threshold issue, troubled us. Could any defendant, much less Michael Anderson, receive a fair trial when a jury would be called upon to hear evidence and deliberate on twenty-two distinct charges, many of which were allegations about unrelated places, times, and events? Wouldn't the mere accumulation of charges and evidence produce a presumption of guilt? Wouldn't a juror naturally believe Anderson to be guilty on count seventeen, for example, simply because they believed him to be guilty on counts ten to fifteen? If Anderson robbed a motel clerk in Pasco on a given night, isn't it likely that the black man of similar description who robbed another motel clerk a week later was, in fact, the same man, regardless of the existence of other proof? As lawyers, our job was to make sure the jury focused honestly and independently on each charge without being unduly influenced by the multiplicity of charges or the temptation to think the defendant must be guilty of everything solely because he was guilty of something. Among other things, we were not about to let the police or prosecutor pin criminal conduct on Michael Anderson simply because he was a convenient and timely target. We were also troubled by what appeared to be a case of overcharging in violation of the double jeopardy clause of the US Constitution. Our concern was that Anderson had been charged in Franklin County on the basis of conduct for which he had already been prosecuted in Benton County.

So, in addition to a change of venue request, Tim and I knew we had to persuade the court to divide the case into two or three separate legal proceedings. We would also scrutinize the allegations, the evidence, and the legal precedent to determine if we might bring a motion attacking the prosecution's effort to double dip.

* * * **

Walla Walla is east of the Tri-Cities in a fertile valley situated below the Blue Mountains. It is a short forty-minute drive. You follow the Columbia to where it is joined at Wallula by the Walla Walla River that trickles westward out of the mountains. Then you go left. Wallula is lost in history except for a big pulp mill that continues to operate in the area. The town now consists of a post office and wrecking yard. It was once a terminal for the Northern Pacific Railroad as the railroad moved west before establishing a new terminal in Pasco. Before that, Lewis and Clark had encamped at Wallula on the expedition's eastward journey. Before that, it was a home to countless generations of natives whose culture barely survived the consequences of Lewis and Clark's stopover.

I always liked the drive because the land is unpopulated and conjures imagery of the Old West. It also evoked memories of my youth—of ski trips and family trips to a funky old cabin on Langdon Lake in the Blue Mountains and what it means to engage in the unvarnished world of unskilled blue-collar labor.

I once worked at the Wallula pulp mill for about two weeks when I was eighteen and just out of high school. To my late adolescent mind, the work was inhumanly demanding, so much so that it appeared to tax even the grizzled old union guys who had worked there for years. I came home after my shifts completely exhausted, demoralized and in pain, my hands cut by crisp, razor-sharp sheets of paper and cardboard spit in relentless succession from the jaws of huge machines that roared at me as I tried to stack the endless product on moving pallets. I was lucky, though—the union voted to strike just a few weeks after I went to work, and I was spared the embarrassment of quitting. The job is an enduring memory for two reasons: it added to my motivation to get a college degree, and it helped me appreciate and respect the lives of those who toil behind the scenes to produce the bounty of material things I sometimes take for granted.

Tim and I drove my black 1978 T-Top Mustang II along the river and talked about the upcoming meeting with Michael at the state penitentiary in Walla Walla. It would be our first visit with our new client, an opportunity to get to know him and to get a sense of how he might wish to be defended on the charges against him. He would be called upon to enter a plea in a few days, usually a perfunctory matter involving the entry of a not-guilty plea so that the lawyers could study the case, decide on a strategy, and prepare for trial. It did not mean there would be a trial. Defendants often enter a plea at some later point before trial after bargaining with the prosecutor for an acceptable deal.

We had read the pleadings and had received copies of basic police reports, including Michael Anderson's signed statement confessing to several of the alleged crimes—the statement he had signed in Seattle after being arrested by the SWAT team. We wondered—would Michael even cooperate with us? Would the fact that he was already sentenced to life terms in prison make him indifferent to the new charges? Was his confession coerced? Did the charges accurately reflect the crimes he committed and his degree of culpability? And what about the alleged crimes to which he did not confess? Were assaults, rapes, and robberies thrown into the overall mix of charges not because there was evidence to support them but simply because Anderson was an easy target?

The penitentiary is located just west and north of downtown Walla Walla. The city has the charm of a conservative and quiet old agricultural center. In 1979, it was surrounded by wheat fields, peas, and onions. Today, the town has become known for grapes and wineries. Whitman College, a fine private liberal arts college, boasts a collection of splendid neoclassical buildings sprinkled around acres of grass and a wandering creek that flows through the campus near the center of town. But you do not need to visit downtown Walla Walla if you are going to the "Hill." Instead, you exit the highway on the town's west side and maneuver through an industrial area, on dirty back roads, for a mile or so, until the high prison walls and guard towers emerge on a slight hill that gives the prison a commanding spot in an uninteresting part of town. The Washington State Penitentiary was built in 1886 and reinforces the stereotyped and brutal look of prisons featured in old movies. It is heavy with brick and stone, protected by towers and catwalks, and unapproachable except by fixed and limited routes. It is a medieval-looking fortress, with all the implications suggested by that image. It is not a fun place to visit and my memories of this and later visits are gloomy indeed.

We parked in the designated lot below the prison and walked up to the first checkpoint, where we presented our credentials. We were sent on to a second checkpoint, where we were body searched and told to wait for a guard to guide us through a maze of metal doors and hallways, across open spaces and gun towers, to a maximum-security visiting room where we could see our client through a plexiglass window and speak to him by telephone.

Michael was already there when we arrived at the designated room. He was dressed in blue jeans and a sweatshirt, clothes he presumably had brought with him or acquired from prison vendors. The baggy clothes did not conceal the man's compelling physical presence, his athletic build, or his chiseled good looks. He sat quietly, motionless, and stared at us, barely nodding in acknowledgement that we were there. The man described by the press as impulsive, predatory, and violent was passive but attentive. I picked up the phone and he did the same.

I began, "Mr. Anderson, I'm George Critchlow and this is my colleague, Tim Mahoney. As you know, we were appointed by the court to represent you. I hope we can spend some time today getting to know you and getting an idea of how you might like us to defend you."

Anderson said nothing for several seconds. Tim and I waited. Finally, keeping his eyes on us, he spoke into the phone. "So, you finally get to meet the monster. I have been wanting to see you. Have you talked to my girlfriend, Dee?"

His voice was soft, his demeanor calm and composed. His teeth were bright and flawless. He was clean-shaven with high cheekbones and a sculpted chin. I did not sense the presence of a monster. I knew that sociopaths come in different shapes and sizes and often come across as attractive and charming, and I knew that Michael might very well be artful at camouflage, but there was something about him that disarmed me immediately. At the same time, the intensity of his physical presence and his watchfulness, even across the glass, were undeniable.

"No, would you like us to?" I said.

"Yes, she is having a hard time, and I want you to help her."

I wanted to encourage him, but I did not want to create unrealistic expectations. "Of course, we can speak with her and let her know we are representing you. Maybe she can help establish an alibi on some of the crimes you are charged with. And we can convey information from you. I am not sure there is much more we can do."

"Well, she is hurting, and she has the children, you know . . . and some legal problems. Anything you can do to help . . ." He did not seem eager to talk about his own legal situation.

Tim took the phone. "Did you receive a copy of the Franklin County Information?" he asked, referring to the legal name for the charging document that set forth the twenty-two criminal counts. "We want to make sure you understand the charges, then we can talk about what you want to do. Our recommendation is that you plead not guilty at next week's arraignment, and then we can figure out how to defend the individual charges or negotiate an appropriate deal if that is your desire."

"There ain't going to be no guilty plea," he replied. "They waited a year to charge me after telling me there would be no new charges if I pled guilty in Benton County. I gave them what they wanted, got four life terms. I'm here—where they wanted me to be. They set me up. There ain't going to be no plea."

"You did sign a confession," Tim reminded him. "That and your pleas of guilty in Benton County pretty much seal your fate on the Franklin County kidnapping charges. We're not saying you should plead to anything, but we need to know if you want us to explore a deal where some charges might be dismissed in exchange for a plea of guilty on others."

Michael's reply was even more emphatic.

"There ain't going to be no plea of guilty, no plea deal. Not only did they lie to me, they put some charges on me in these new papers that I got nothing to do with. I don't know what they're talking about."

I took the phone back from Tim. "Okay, Mr. Anderson, we will get to work on possible defenses and will assume we are going to trial. We represent you and will consult you on all important decisions. There are some things we would like to do strategically—things like changing venue and dividing the case into two or three different proceedings. But you will be involved in everything. We can visit with you when they transport you to Pasco for all court proceedings, and we can always drive over here to the penitentiary as well."

We spent some time talking about Anderson's views on a change of venue and splitting the case into separate trials. We did not talk about the charges related to the Pasco home invasion, tying up the children and father, or the kidnapping and assault of the mother who was taken as a hostage to Seattle. We chatted instead about an assortment of unrelated charges—allegations of serious crimes that took place in the Pasco area shortly before Anderson was arrested on the Safeway robbery and his subsequent escape from the Franklin County Jail. Anderson was cooperative but perfunctory.

"I know nothing about those crimes," he said. "And how can anyone expect me to remember where I was on specific days or nights a year and a half ago? Let them try to prove it."

Before we left, I said, "Mr. Anderson, we will do everything we can to help you. In the meantime, how are you getting along here at the penitentiary? Is there anything you need?"

His answer came from the depths of his experience behind bars. "It's a prison. I'll survive. The inmates can get me anything I need. Tell Dee I'm okay. And you can call me Michael. I mean, you dudes can't be much older than me." He smiled, not a broad smile or an inappropriate smile, just a smile. It surprised me, as did his next comment:, "I hear your dad knows his way around the courtroom. There's lots of guys here from the Tri-Cities. He gonna be working for me too?"

I deflected. "I occasionally have a beer with him. He'll be around."

Our visit was ending. We said our goodbyes. He paused before hanging up the phone.

"Every day I think about what I done to that poor woman, the lady from Pasco with the family. I will have to live with that until I die."

Was this comment meant to curry favor with Tim and me? Was it calculating and manipulative? Or was it an expression of real remorse, perhaps an unburdening?

Michael was taken by a guard down a long gray hall. He would return to days of deadening loneliness and monotony broken by random violence. He would watch prisoners throw themselves from upper tiers or slash their wrists. It was a world designed to remind him of his shame. He was home again, a place with no mirrors, no self, where a prisoner's identity was meant to dissolve and disappear into a cesspool of lost souls who believed themselves unworthy. It would not be long before he started shooting heroin to kill the pain. He could not, would not escape. His road was as dark as it had ever been. And it still had no turns.

Tim and I left the prison and found a local pub. We sipped beers and talked casually about the Supersonics' chances to win the NBA championship next month. Downtown Freddy Brown, Gus Williams, Jack Sikma. This could be the year! There was no discussion about what had just been confirmed—we would spend the next few months preparing to defend a case we could not possibly win. We were going to trial on behalf of a man who almost everyone feared and reviled.

We drove back to the Tri-Cities and followed the twisting Walla Walla River, as I mentally navigated a maze of different thoughts and feelings. My meeting with Michael and my understanding of the depressing world he returned to left me feeling vaguely guilty about sifting through the comparatively painless complications of my own life. No matter, my issues were real and irrepressible. They demanded some attention.

I was dating different women at the time, an emotionally awkward and logistically challenging pattern that shielded me from real intimacy for years to come. I had other cases set for trial and wondered if there would be enough hours in the day to get everything done. The aftershocks of my parent's recent divorce, although decreasing in number, were still capable of rattling me and my relations with my four strong-minded siblings.

My parents had been married for thirty-five years. I have already mentioned that my dad typified World War II veterans who rarely talked about their combat experience. He could speak effusively about law, politics, race, and Christ's Sermon on the Mount, but he did not easily share his emotions or vulnerabilities. He was both transparent and opaque. Mom, like Dad, was a political progressive, and she was warm and engaging—an accomplished conversationalist who made people feel comfortable. She was, however, less open and relaxed in talking about the cultural and lifestyle changes that grew out of the 1960s and 1970s when her children came of age. She could not be described as New Age. It was difficult for her to discuss sex, alternative spiritual paths, or new approaches to diet and health. She was a strong woman who rarely disclosed her insecurities, and she was a confounding mix of openness, good cheer, and puritanism.

Mom and Dad had abundant lives, rich family traditions, an extensive network of friends, a history of civic involvement, and a commitment to nonprofit service and the Episcopal Church. But they lacked the communication and relationship skills necessary to overcome my dad's workaholism, an empty nest, financial pressures, and in-law distractions. Toward the end of the marriage, my father became a bit of a philanderer, which all but guaranteed a marital collapse. While my relationship with my father continued to grow, this was not the case with a couple of my sisters. It took me years before I understood how my parents' marriage and my father's intimacy issues were echoed in my own life and relationships.

Another recurrent thought came to mind as Tim and I ended our trip to the penitentiary. It was not so much a thought as a sensation, a familiar and steady pull, inborn and ineffable, like the force that guides the needle of a compass. It signaled a beckoning world and all the stimulating and exotic possibilities that lay beyond the Tri-Cities. I could not shake the feeling that I would someday need to chart a new course.

I also ruminated on the curious convergence of my professional journey and Michael Anderson's dark road. Something had transpired in our meeting that transcended my expectations and professional duties. It was not a *Casablanca* moment where I inferred the beginning of a beautiful friendship, but there was a real sense that we had something to share beyond the need to exchange information for strictly legal purposes. There was a nebulous, embryonic human connection. Michael Anderson did not scare me. He intrigued me.

Chapter 22

"Judge: 'Miss West, are you trying to show contempt for this court?'
Mae West: 'On the contrary, your honor, I was doin' my best to hide it.'"

—Trial Transcript

I was not an especially experienced or polished trial attorney when I was appointed to represent Michael. On the other hand, I was no neophyte and I had learned from a fine lawyer, one of the best trial lawyers around. On my first day of work in November 1977, my father admonished me for coming in so late. It was eight AM. In my world, that was early—especially since I had just returned from a three-month odyssey, following law school, to several Aegean islands where eight AM could very well mark the end of the previous night rather than the beginning of a new day. Dad gave me a thin file containing a few notes and asked me to interview a potential client in a local jail. The inmate had been arrested over the weekend, and a family member had contacted our law firm for possible representation.

The need to make a jail visit did not bother me on my first day of work. I had the benefit of clinical training in law school, where, under faculty supervision, I represented several clients in both civil and criminal matters. I had interviewed clients and witnesses, filed complaints and motions, conducted discovery, negotiated settlements, and even tried a case to a jury. Teaching these skills later became the core of my work and career as a law school professor. No, what bothered me on that fall morning was not the challenge of my first interview as a licensed lawyer—it was the prickly recognition that getting up early and doing serious work was my new and ongoing reality.

With the thin file in hand, I made my way to the jail around nine AM—still early by my calculation. As I arrived, I observed a throng of news reporters. The jail was part of a larger complex of municipal offices, judicial offices, and courtrooms. An event of some public or political importance was evidently in progress. I found the jail administrator

PART 4: DUE PROCESS AND EQUAL PROTECTION

and announced my purpose and the name of the inmate I hoped to see. The name no sooner passed my lips then the press smothered me, asking questions and demanding answers. My father had said nothing about the nature of the charge, and I assumed I was visiting a client arrested for something relatively minor such as a driving or low-level drug offense. The situation obviously involved something more serious. The reporters and newscasters wanted to know if my supposed client would be pleading guilty, why he had slit the victim's throat, if drugs were involved, and how it felt to represent a murderer.

Of course, my father knew the alleged crime when he handed me the file. He had sent me on a task that would usually be reserved for a more experienced lawyer. I felt empowered and validated. And a bit overwhelmed.

Eight months later, after hundreds of hours of legal research, investigation, brainstorming, and briefing, my father and I tried the murder case to a jury. In appearance and style, Dad was a cross between Gregory Peck playing Atticus Finch in *To Kill a Mockingbird* and Spencer Tracy playing the Clarence Darrow-based character in *Inherit the Wind*. He had a thick mane of white hair, a handsome face, abundant hoary eyebrows, and a gravelly voice that gave him an advantage over courtroom adversaries whose visage and demeanor were more forgettable.

In closing argument, Dad stood up and began his address to the jury, "I don't know why my son has referred to me as 'Mr. Critchlow' during the entire course of this trial. I'm his father and he could have just called me Dad."

That simple statement ingratiated my father to both me and the jury and forged in me an appreciation for talking plainly and honestly to jurors. The jury returned a not-guilty verdict. I, *we*, had won my first trial—a murder trial!

People inquired, of course, whether I believed the client to be truly innocent. Some people forget that a not-guilty verdict is different from a declaration of innocence. Not guilty means the prosecution lacked proof beyond a reasonable doubt. My answer to the question in this and other cases was that I subscribe to the constitutional rules of law that say the accused in a criminal case is presumed innocent, has a right to counsel, a right to confront witnesses, and cannot be subjected to jail or worse if there is a reasonable doubt about his or her guilt.

There was a time when my commitment to these principles was shaken. I received a phone call from a sobbing woman in the middle of the night several years after I started practicing law. She identified herself as the woman I had cross-examined in a rape trial some years before. She had been the alleged victim of a forcible rape at knifepoint after a home invasion at her apartment. My client claimed the sex was consensual and the woman had concocted a story of rape only after the sexual encounter was discovered by the woman's boyfriend. I remembered the case vividly, including my effort to discredit the woman's testimony.

"How do you feel now, Mr. Big Shot lawyer?" bellowed the woman. "Does it make you feel powerful?"

She was angry, caustic, and clearly channeling feelings from her experience as a victim witness. But I had no idea what had triggered this phone call so long after that trial. She continued for a bit, ranting about me and the justice system.

"I remember you, but what's going on? Why are you calling me?" I finally interjected.

She screamed, "Your wonderful, *innocent* client just got arrested again. You want to know the charge? First degree rape at knifepoint in a woman's apartment!"

I was genuinely upset by the news. The pain of the woman on the phone hit me in the gut, which was some distance from where I stored legal information about criminal procedure. While my belief in the constitutional rights for all people accused of crimes has never wavered, I learned there can be an emotional price paid by lawyers who serve the lofty principles of due process, liberty, and client loyalty.

* * * *

Mahoney and I knew we had a problem when *State v. Anderson* was assigned for trial. Judge Yencopal had generously given Anderson two court-appointed lawyers, but the case was then transferred to Judge Fred Frederick for trial. Frederick was the judge who had presided over the 1978 Benton County charges that resulted in a plea of guilty and the imposition of four life sentences. He was the first judge to go on record recommending that Anderson be kept behind bars for the remainder of his natural days. Not only did we not want Frederick on the Franklin County case, we did not want any local judge on the case for the same reason we did not want a local jury. Everyone knew about Anderson and knew he had already pled guilty in the 1978 prosecution. We had to assume everyone had already formed an opinion about his guilt. We also assumed every local judge would be predisposed to impose the most draconian sentence in the likely event Anderson was convicted on any of the pending twenty-two charges.

We quickly arranged for Judge Frederick to be taken off the case. Washington law allowed for the disqualification of an assigned judge based on the filing of a simple affidavit alleging judicial prejudice. The disqualification was automatic and could not be contested by the prosecutor or the judge himself. However, the law also limited a party to just one such "affidavit of prejudice." Any subsequent allegation of prejudice against another judge had to be proved by evidence that showed actual prejudice—a difficult burden. Judges rarely admitted to prejudice.

Tim Mahoney filed the affidavit of prejudice as to Frederick and the case was then assigned to Judge Knight. We were unable to locate any evidence that documented or intimated that the judge was biased against our client. There were no publicly reported comments and we had no private information that might enable us to support a challenge to the judge's impartiality. Still, we believed it would be tantamount to malpractice to allow the case to be heard by Judge Knight or any other local judge. We decided not to challenge the judge directly. We opted instead for a strategy that rested on our belief that the court would have to change venue of the case in order to secure an impartial jury. If the venue was changed to a new county, a new judge from that county would presumably preside over the case.

By late April 1979 we had filed a motion to change venue supported by dozens of attached newspaper articles, editorial opinions, and transcriptions of television news reports relating to Anderson. The amount of publicity and its inflammatory nature seemed to compel the conclusion that Anderson could not get a fair trial in Franklin County. If Judge Knight disagreed, we were prepared to take it up with the Court of Appeals.

As sometimes happens in litigation, the judge found a way to give with one hand what he took away with the other. At the scheduled hearing on the matter, we argued what appeared to be plain and indisputable statutory law. But Judge Knight was cagey.

"Well, maybe you know more about the law than I do, counsel, but I doubt it. There is no way to know what the legislature meant when it passed the change of venue law. Unless you can bring me clear authority to support your position, I am not going to order a change of venue. I will, however, move the trial to another county so we can get jurors who are not tainted by pretrial publicity. But I will continue to preside."

Tim Mahoney waited patiently while I squirmed. The judge finished and Tim urged the judge to reconsider his analysis, "Your honor, with all due respect, there is no authority for trying this case outside of Franklin County except under the Change of Venue statute. And that statute has always required the entire case be removed to a new county. The new county is then responsible for assigning one of its judges. Not only is that contemplated by the clear language of the statute, it has been the custom and practice in Washington."

"Perhaps it is custom, Mr. Mahoney, but it is not required. There is no reason we cannot borrow a courtroom and jurors in, say, Spokane County and all of us will simply drive up there and try this thing."

Mahoney took a deep breath and continued with a line of argument we hoped would not be necessary.

"Frankly, Judge, we do not believe Mr. Anderson can get a fair trial with any Franklin County judge, including yourself. We are not suggesting that you are biased against our client in any conscious way—only that it would be impossible for any judge to be immune from the massive publicity and public animosity engendered by the case. A true change of venue would accomplish what, under the circumstances, our client is entitled to—an impartial judge and jury."

Judge Knight's voice rose. He leaned forward as if to add physical force to what he was about to say. "Let the record reflect that I take great umbrage at the suggestion that I am unable to be fair and impartial in this matter. Counsel will refrain from making any such unsubstantiated allegation. I would refer you to the lawyer code of ethics, which prohibits a lawyer from impugning the court's integrity. My decision will stand. The clerk will investigate possible locations for trial, and counsel will be notified of further arrangements. Trial is scheduled for June 26."

We were, of course, happy to have the trial moved to a new location. But Judge Knight's decision to stay on the case spelled disaster. Our trial strategy depended on our ability to persuade a judge to dismiss certain charges, exclude certain evidence, and instruct the jury that our client may have committed certain crimes, but those crimes were less serious than the ones charged. We also hoped to have the case broken into two separate jury trials. We did not trust Judge Knight to be open to any these requests.

Later that evening, Tim joined me at the law firm library for a beer. I hoped to bring my father into the conversation.

"Why do you suppose the judge is so determined to keep this case?" I asked. "You would think he would jump at the chance to dump it on another judge in another county."

Tim was blunt. "Two reasons. One, he hates our client and, two, he loves the publicity. He wants to get credit for putting Michael away for a very long time."

"Christ, he's already doing back-to-back life terms. You'd think they got their pound of flesh and a lot more."

My father walked into the library, headed straight to the wet bar, and poured himself a Ballantine's scotch on the rocks. "How goes the battle?" he inquired.

"Not great, Dad. Judge Knight says we can go to a different county to try the case, but he's going with us as judge."

"Kind of unusual isn't it?"

"It's not legal. It's manipulative and reversible."

Dad paused and considered his words. "It may be reversible, but you should not expect to get the appellate court to intervene before trial. Plus, the judge can probably get to the same result without breaking the law."

"What do you mean?"

"Well, it seems to me the judge could simply change venue under the statute and then ask the court in the new venue to invite him to sit on the case. Judges visit other counties all the time."

I looked at Tim. He sipped his beer and said, "Hadn't thought of that. We may be stuck with the arrogant prig."

My father grinned. "Ah, you just have to know how to handle him. Massage his ego. Of course, it would be an easier road if your client wasn't black."

Chapter 23

"In all criminal prosecutions, the accused shall enjoy the right to . . . an impartial jury."

—Sixth Amendment, US Constitution

Consistent with Anderson's instructions, there would be no plea. Tim and I prepared for trial knowing the main evidence against our client would be his own confession and the testimony of victims who had been seriously hurt and emotionally scarred. We focused on defenses that highlighted the prosecutor's propensity to be greedy—to charge more and greater offenses than were warranted by the facts. In our opinion, the facts supported lesser charges of unlawful imprisonment and theft rather than the more serious charges of kidnapping and robbery. We also took issue with the burglary charge on the theory that Michael's entry into the home constituted trespass, a misdemeanor.

Success or failure would not change Michael's life for the next few decades, but if we succeeded there could be a chance he might someday be paroled.

* * * *

Judge Knight took the bench to begin the trial on a fine, sunny day in June. We were in the grand old Spokane County Courthouse on Broadway, a few blocks northwest of downtown Spokane. Like the Franklin County Courthouse in Pasco, it was a Renaissance design rooted in the sixteenth century. However, it drew from the architectural history of French castles rather than the lineage of Italian palaces. It was a romantic building distinguished by towers and turrets and decorative arches. Built in the 1890s, it represented Spokane's desire to stimulate both community pride and a faltering economy that followed the city's early boomtown years. It served as the center for judicial and other county business. In the early years, it was also the venue for public hangings.

PART 4: DUE PROCESS AND EQUAL PROTECTION

Spokane is 130 miles north of the Tri-Cities and about 100 miles south of the Canadian border. It is the largest city in eastern Washington, owing to a history of mining, forest products, agriculture, and, since World War II, a major Air Force base. It was conservative and provincial, at least until it sponsored a World's Fair in 1974, an event that caused some constituents to visualize a future of cultural and environmental progress, economic growth, and an ability to compete with Seattle's relative sophistication and prosperity. Indeed, forty years later, Spokane's manageable size, cost of living, and economic opportunity have made it an attractive alternative to Seattle's inflated prices and urban congestion. At the time of the trial, the city was only slightly more diverse than the Tri-Cities. There were pockets of African Americans who had migrated north earlier in the century, some Hispanics, and urban American Indians whose histories were tied to the many tribes that populated eastern Washington, North Idaho, and western Montana—the Spokanes, Kalispels, Coeur d'Alenes, Salish-Kootenai, Yakamas, Colvilles, and Nez Perce. Tim and I had attended law school in Spokane and were familiar with the city's charms as well as the cultural peculiarities of a community nestled in the inland northwest near north Idaho.

The judge announced the first order of business. He wanted to settle the question of the trial's venue under applicable Washington law.

"Counsel, we are now ensconced here in the Spokane County Courthouse—a beautiful courthouse with a wonderful group of county employees who will undoubtedly attend to all of our needs. However, I have been thinking about the technical arguments previously raised by Mr. Anderson's lawyers regarding the need to follow the change of venue statute. Of course, it was never my desire to circumvent the law. I simply felt it was preferable for me to stay on as judge even as the case itself was to be tried outside of Franklin County. Having now had a chance to look more closely at the issue, I have determined that Mr. Anderson's counsel are correct. We can only be in Spokane County on a change of venue. I am now signing a court order officially changing venue to Spokane. As to who will preside over the case, you should know that the Spokane judges have invited me to handle the matter. I have been denominated as a 'visiting' judge."

My father had been right. With a stroke of the pen, Judge Knight had retained power over the case while eliminating grounds for an appeal by Anderson.

A jury panel of several dozen Spokane County residents was then ushered into the courtroom to go through the jury selection process known as *voir dire*. They were almost all white and evenly divided in gender. Prospective jurors would be called at random by a court clerk and each would be subject to questioning by the court and the parties' lawyers, to determine if they could be fair and impartial if selected to sit on the jury. Defense lawyers know this is an important part of any criminal trial. Not only did it offer the defense an opportunity to get to know a juror's background and thinking, it could be used to humanize the defendant and plant seeds of doubt about the sufficiency of the prosecutor's case. We were seeking to seat jurors who had open minds, who were reasonably well-educated, who were not racist, and who would listen carefully to the evidence before deciding exactly what crimes, if any, were proved beyond a reasonable doubt.

Judge Knight introduced himself, the prosecuting attorney and his assistant, Tim Mahoney, and me. He did not introduce the defendant in any conventional sense. Rather, he told the jury the name of the case, *State of Washington vs. Michael Dwayne Anderson*, and informed the jury panel that the defendant was seated next to his attorneys. He then recited the names of expected witnesses and asked the panel if anyone knew anyone on the list. Hearing no response, the judge addressed a matter that rarely comes up in an American criminal case. He had decided to "quarantine" the selected jury for the full length of the trial to prevent jurors from being exposed to or contaminated by publicity or other outside influences. He explained that such a step was taken only in the most "notorious" cases where there was a likelihood of substantial publicity and public attention. The selected jury would be housed at the Ridpath Hotel in downtown Spokane. They would eat together, be transported back and forth from court together, and be under constant supervision by court personnel.

"I know this will be a burden to many of you with spouses and families," the judge explained. "I would not take this measure, a measure that adds significantly to the cost of trial, unless I was sure it is necessary."

Tim and I had mixed feelings about the quarantine order. We did fear the possibility that local publicity would adversely affect the jury. We also knew that a jury cut off from family, work, and normal routines could become impatient and anxious during a prolonged trial. Some jurors might blame their discomfort on the defendant. Also, since Tim and I would be staying at the same hotel as the jurors, we would need to be especially careful not to talk about the case in restaurants and public settings where jurors might be present.

Before the court clerk called the names of prospective jurors, I registered a formal objection to the way Spokane County selected jurors from a master list of potential jurors. Under the Constitution, criminal defendants were entitled to a jury selected from a fair cross-section of the community. The jury panel that showed up in this case was comprised almost exclusively of white people. It did not include a representative proportion of Spokane County's minority community. I argued that the panel was comprised of people identified by reference only to voter registration rolls, an inherently inadequate means for ensuring fair representation of rich and poor, white and people of color, property owners and renters, old and young. Many people did not register to vote, especially American Indians, many African Americans, and young people. Although the law was not entirely clear at the time, some court opinions declared a constitutional preference for multiple sources—driver's license and state identification card lists and telephone books as well as voter registration records. As expected, Judge Knight summarily denied my request for a more inclusive jury panel, and he opined that Spokane County had a fine system for gathering jurors.

A court clerk picked the names of thirteen prospective jurors to come forward and sit in the jury box for questioning. All were white. None had heard of the case. About six of the jurors expressed reluctance to sit on a jury that would be quarantined. Judge Knight stated that he empathized with them but reminded them that jury duty was so important it could not be excused except for the most compelling reasons. A few jurors had such reasons—care for a sick or disabled family member, a planned and paid-for upcoming trip to Europe. The judge summarized the nature of the charges, explained that the trial would last approximately three or four days, and then turned the questioning over to the lawyers, with the prosecutor going first.

The prosecutor was neither old nor young, not especially charismatic, but not off-putting. He was experienced and business like. His dialogue with potential jurors was direct and professional. He did not have to go out of his way to demonize Anderson. He simply made repeated references to the multiple charges as a way of letting the jury know the prosecution regarded the defendant as a monster. The case was a slam dunk and he knew there was no need for argument or emotion during the jury selection process.

Tim and I asked questions that needed to be asked at the risk of alienating or offending. We wanted to know if the mere fact that a young black man was charged with violent offenses automatically created an impression of guilt. We asked about what books and newspapers and magazines the individuals read, what television shows they watched, what organizations and churches they associated with, and how they felt, in general, about the courts and the justice system. The judge permitted us to ask direct questions as to whether a prospective juror was racially biased—something that almost all people would respond to in the negative—but would not allow us to ask questions that might indirectly probe the same subject.

"Mr. Thompson, I am happy to hear that you have no inclination to hold my client's race against him," I said to the first person selected for questioning. "I wonder, though, if you might share with us your opinion on matters such as affirmative action or mandatory busing of school children to achieve integration?"

The court cut me off. "Mr. Critchlow, it is inappropriate for you to ask about personal political opinions or attitudes. After all, these jurors have some right to privacy. The man has already told us he is not racially prejudiced. Now move on."

We pursued other strategies designed to penetrate a juror's false fidelity to what today would be called political correctness. Our objective was to make it easier for people to publicly admit to racial bias.

Tim Mahoney asked another potential juror, "Please tell us about your experience with people who are not Caucasian. Do you have friends or colleagues who are black or Hispanic?"

Such a question typically elicited an eager and positive response. Oh yes, people knew a person of color when they were in the military, or they worked with a person born in Mexico, or they interacted with someone in college who had dark skin. One panel member described her friendship with a white couple who had actually adopted a black child.

As the *voir dire* process dragged on, the judge became impatient, and prospective jurors who had not yet been questioned learned what was to come from listening to the earlier questions and answers. Most panel members wanted to serve, and even those who were reluctant wanted to be perceived as fair-minded and impartial. *Voir dire* educated them as to how they should answer awkward questions so as to avoid saying something that might disqualify them from jury service.

Tim and I did not expect to seat a jury that was completely free from racial animus, conscious or unconscious. We were realistic enough to know that very few people are immune from the suspicion that people of other races have unfavorable characteristics or attitudes. What we wanted was for someone to simply and honestly acknowledge that fact. We hoped to use an example of such candor as an opportunity to encourage jurors to examine their own hearts and, if chosen to sit on the jury, to consciously monitor their thinking and their assumptions to assure that Michael Anderson was not being judged based on his color. In short, we wanted an example that would elevate a jury's better angels and cause it to bend over backwards in an effort to be fair to our client. We finally struck gold.

I had questioned juror number nine about his background, his associations, and his general attitudes about race and the justice system. He was a Korean War Veteran and had grown up in a small town in North Idaho. Like the other jurors, he assured me he had no problems sitting on a jury involving a black man charged with serious and violent offenses. He also assured me he absolutely accepted and believed in the proposition that a person charged with a crime is presumed innocent. Juror number nine thought the American system of justice was just about the best in the world. And there was no place for racial bias because everyone was entitled to equal justice.

I was getting tense. Up until now, I felt the *voir dire* process had been largely a rhetorical exercise where everyone played a role and said what was expected based on some idealized notion of how the American justice system was supposed to work. There was something about juror number nine—his eagerness to please, his pat answers, mixed together with his evident and powerful sense of patriotism—that made me think he could be the example we were looking for.

"Mr. Simpson, thank you for your answers and your patience in sitting through this prolonged jury selection process," I said to juror number nine. "I know you recognize how important it is for jurors to be forthcoming and honest in this process. Am I correct?"

"Absolutely," Mr. Simpson replied.

"And do you understand that we cannot provide the kind of justice we are proud of in this country if jurors do not share their true feelings, even if doing so is awkward or embarrassing?"

"Well, yes, I think I understand that."

I continued with one eye on the judge, knowing his desire to keep me on a short leash.

"What I mean, Mr. Simpson, is that if someone really wanted to sit on a jury, maybe because they thought it would be an interesting civic experience, they might be tempted to say the kinds of things that are expected even if those things were not entirely true. But, do you agree that such a juror would not be doing his duty to the American justice system and would not, in fact, be acting in a very patriotic fashion?"

I heard the sound of the judge's gavel and turned to see Judge Knight's face, contorted and flushed.

"That will be enough, Mr. Critchlow. I will not have you questioning these jurors' patriotism."

"I understand, your honor. With all due respect, I am not questioning anyone's patriotism. I am simply equating patriotism with duty. In any event, I have only one final question of Mr. Simpson if the court would allow me the discretion."

"Yes, well, make it quick. I would like to get jury selection out of the way."

Judge Knight was impatient. He wanted an efficient, streamlined trial, but he also suspected lawyers, especially criminal defense lawyers, would take advantage of any opportunity to influence jurors in manipulative ways.

"Mr. Simpson," I continued, "I have one last question. Knowing what you know about the importance of candor and duty in the criminal justice process, can you state whether you would want someone such as yourself sitting on the jury if you were Mr. Anderson?"

Mr. Simpson paused, looked down, looked at his fellow panel members, and turned back to me. He spoke clearly and directly. "No, I would not want someone such a myself sitting on a jury if I was your client."

"And why is that, Mr. Simpson?" I asked.

He answered, again in a clear, straightforward manner.

"Because, as soon as I walked into the courtroom this morning and saw Mr. Anderson sitting there, saw that he was a black man, I assumed he was guilty. I think he is entitled to jurors who do not share my prejudice."

I thanked Mr. Simpson for his honesty. The judge also thanked him and told him he was discharged from jury duty. The court then recessed for lunch. By late afternoon, we had seated twelve jurors and one alternate. They were all white. I hoped Mr. Simpson's honest and courageous admission would embolden the jury to be the best they could be.

Chapter 24

"Four things belong to a judge: to hear courteously, to answer wisely, to consider soberly, and to decide impartially."

—Socrates

The Spokane jury was visibly shaken by the testimony of Mrs. Carlson. She narrated a tale of terror that most people only read about or experience in movies or bad dreams. The story was elicited by the prosecutor in excruciating and painful detail. A quivering voice and occasional sob were all that could be heard in the hushed courtroom. The jury heard most of it—the encounter with a stranger in a dark basement, the pistol-whipping and kicking, the seizure and binding of her children and husband, the fear of her family's imminent death, her abduction, confinement in the trunk of her own car, the prolonged and anxious ride to Seattle, and the final fraught moments tied together with the Giant T manager in a Seattle hotel room. She said nothing about a sexual assault.

This was not the first trial where Michael had to listen to testimony about how he had hurt people. But it was evident he was deeply ashamed of hurting Mrs. Carlson. He slumped in his chair holding his downturned face in his hands. He did not look at the witness and she did not, could not, look at him. Tim Mahoney and I tried to affect the manner of responsible professionals who were sensitive to the emotional weight of the testimony but unaffected by its legal significance.

Judge Knight recessed the trial twice to permit Mrs. Carlson and shaken jurors to collect themselves. Emotional discomfort is a familiar by-product of courtroom drama. In this case, it was much exacerbated by the fact that Mrs. Carlson's ordeal as a witness caused her twice to be seized by uncontrollable episodes of hyperventilation.

When the prosecutor finished questioning the witness, there was no cross-examination. Trial lawyers almost always cross-examine damaging witnesses to reduce the impact of their testimony. Sometimes it is just not appropriate. Here, Mrs. Carlson's credibility was not in dispute. Michael had fully confessed, and parts of that confession had already been read to the jury by a Seattle police detective who testified to the aftermath of Anderson's arrest by the Seattle SWAT team. Besides, cross-examination would have been unkind to the witness and a tactless adversarial spectacle.

Mr. Carlson was the next witness. We were now in our third day of trial, and the jury was no doubt wondering if and when there might be some showing of a defense against the multiple charges of burglary, kidnapping, robbery, and assault. Tim's opening statement had informed the jury that the defendant did not deny his misdeeds, but also that the defense believed the prosecution had overcharged the case. Several counts had already been withdrawn by the prosecutor. We were now prepared to examine Mr. Carlson on minor factual details that could mean the difference between our client being convicted of serious felonies and lesser offenses. The consequence for Michael could be the difference between years in prison and dying in prison.

Mr. Carlson testified to coming home on the night in question and having a stranger, a young black man, put a gun to his head in the presence of his children. He related how Anderson gagged and bound the family while threatening them with death if they did not obey him. He talked softly about his pain and feelings of impotence at seeing his wife's bruised and bloody face. The jury tracked the testimony with the same solemnity and horror they displayed when listening to his wife. Mr. Carlson concluded by tearfully recounting his fear that he would never see his wife again after she was forced at gunpoint to drive her kidnapper to an unknown destination and an uncertain fate.

Mahoney's cross-examination was focused, genial, and gentle.

"Mr. Carlson, I know this is difficult for you, and I do not intend to keep you on the witness stand too long. However, we do have a few questions that we hope will clarify the facts so that the jury will have a completely accurate picture when they deliberate on the charges against our client. One of the charges is robbery. Could you describe the precise manner in which Mr. Anderson obtained the thirty dollars he took from you?"

Carlson was forthcoming but confused.

"Well, he took the money out of my wallet. Is that what you are getting at?"

"Yes, but could you tell the jury where the wallet was when he took the thirty dollars?"

"On the table."

"And why was it on the table?"

"I had placed it there when the defendant told me to empty my pockets."

Our strategy was to create reasonable doubt on the question of whether this fact constituted the crime of robbery, legally defined as taking property from another by threat or use of force. We believed that the jury should be given the opportunity to convict our client on the lesser crime of misdemeanor theft—defined as taking property valued under $500 from another without his or her consent.

Mahoney continued with his probing. "Mr. Carlson, when did the defendant take possession of the money from your wallet?"

"Just before he left the house."

"And did he point the gun at you or otherwise say he was going to hurt you if you did not let him take the money?"

"Well, I don't really recall. He had a handgun; we all had seen it. But I can't say if he threatened me with it when he took the money. Taking the money just seemed like a convenience, an afterthought. We were all tied up."

"Is it fair, then, to say that Mr. Anderson is a thief?"

"Well, yes, he is at least that."

"And, just to be clear, Mr. Anderson did not take the money from your person. He stole it from your home, correct?"

"I suppose you could say that, yes."

Judge Knight interrupted. "We will now take our noon recess and reconvene at two o'clock. Mr. Mahoney, you may continue your cross-examination after lunch."

Tim and I found a restaurant far from anywhere the jury might be dining. It was a downtown hole in the wall that served breakfast all day. I ordered ham and eggs, Tim a cheeseburger with fries. We fortified ourselves with coffee and conferred quietly about how Tim might continue the cross-examination. He had laid the foundation for us to ask the court to instruct jury members that they could choose to convict Michael of a misdemeanor rather than a felony, a misdemeanor that could be punished by no more than a year in jail. Our plan now was to elicit testimony that would serve as the basis for convicting Anderson of unlawful imprisonment, a lesser offense than the kidnapping with which he was charged. Neither of us were confident the judge would agree.

I tried to be reassuring. "Tying someone up and gagging them in their own home is unlawful imprisonment. It is different from restraining someone and carting them off by force for ransom, torture, or sexual abuse. Otherwise, every unlawful imprisonment would be a kidnapping and there would be no need for two distinct offenses. This is not a crazy defense, and it is one the judge and jury should take seriously."

"I get that, George, but I don't think the judge is going to like where we are going."

"So what? He gets paid to decide difficult legal questions."

"And we get paid to represent criminals. The judge has it easy."

Judge Knight brought the courtroom to order at precisely two PM. Tim proceeded with his cross-examination of Mr. Carlson.

"Now, you have testified that the defendant tore up bed sheets, gagged you, and tied your hands and feet. He apparently did the same with your boys and your wife, is that correct?"

"Yes," Mr. Carlson replied.

"Did he move you from the house?"

"No."

"Did he say anything about holding you hostage?"

"No."

"Did he say anything to you or anyone else, to the best of your knowledge, about holding you for ransom?"

"No."

"Do you believe Mr. Anderson restrained you in order to kill you or make you experience extreme mental distress?"

"I don't know why he tied us up."

"Did he threaten you or your family sexually?"

"No."

"Did the defendant have permission to enter your house?"

"Of course not."

"So, in your opinion, he was a trespasser?"

The prosecutor objected. "Your honor, that calls for a legal conclusion, and this witness is not qualified to make such a conclusion."

Our goal, among others, was to develop evidence of trespass, a misdemeanor, as an alternative to convicting Anderson of the more serious charge of burglary. Burglary required proof that the accused entered a house unlawfully with the intention of committing a felony in the house.

Tim countered the objection. "Your honor, trespass is a common term used by laymen to describe an illegal entry. It is surely not limited to its usage as a legal term of art."

The judge recognized the purpose of Tim's question. "I will allow the question, but you should understand that it is for the court to instruct the jury as to what charges are supported by the evidence."

Tim continued his examination. "Mr. Carlson, do you believe the defendant trespassed when he entered your house and hid in the basement?"

"Absolutely," the witness declared.

"Thank you. No more questions, your honor . . . I apologize, I do have one last question. Mr. Carlson, do you have any evidence or knowledge that the defendant intended to commit a crime in your home when he decided to enter and hide in the basement?"

"I don't know what he intended."

"Thank you. That's all I have."

Tim turned to me, away from the jury, and nodded ever so slightly. It was an acknowledgment that he had succeeded in establishing a basis for instructing the jury that it could find Anderson guilty of misdemeanors and low-grade felonies rather than the serious charges that might lead to multiple life sentences.

Two other witnesses testified briefly following the emotional appearance of Mr. and Mrs. Carlson. A local jail official testified that Michael had been incarcerated at the Franklin County Jail and had escaped not long before he took refuge in the Carlson home. A law enforcement lab technician told the jury that the red stains on Mrs. Carlson's clothes were, in fact, her own blood. The prosecution then rested its case. Now it was our turn and we had little to contribute other than our argument that Anderson was guilty of lesser crimes.

The late afternoon sunlight poured through west-facing windows, adding luster to the courtroom's polished mahogany furnishings and unwelcome warmth to a poorly ventilated faux French castle. Lethargy was now an enemy of a fast-paced trial. Court personnel and jurors were thinking about dinner, their families, and what might be on evening television. The case had proceeded smoothly. Jury selection and the presentation of evidence had been efficient and unimpeded. The prosecution had now rested, and the defense would typically be given an opportunity to fine-tune its strategy and schedule witnesses. It was a logical time to adjourn for the day. But Judge Knight was in a hurry. He wanted to finish the trial as quickly as possible so everyone could go home. He was tired of the Ridpath Hotel, tired of restaurant food, and impatient to return to the comfort and familiarity of his Franklin County manor. Mostly, however, he believed the trial to be a waste of time and taxpayer money.

"Is the defense prepared to call its first witness?" the judge queried.

Tim and I were exhausted and emotionally on edge. We had debated for days whether or not to put our client on the witness stand. If we did, we might personalize him and give him an opportunity to persuade the jury that his crimes were less grave than what was charged. On the other hand, he would inescapably be subjected to a cross-examination we could not control. The prosecutor would grill him on his long history of criminal convictions, his current residence at the state penitentiary, and the brutal details of the crimes charged in this case. Michael was willing to testify because he wanted the jury to know the whole truth and he felt the case against him had in some ways been misrepresented. We advised against it because we feared the impact of cross-examination.

I turned to the judge and advised that we had a couple of witnesses who would be available the next day to testify briefly about some rather minor evidentiary discrepancies.

"Do you intend to put the defendant on the witness stand?'" he asked. "If so, now would be a good time, so let's get on with it."

The question was put to us in front of the jury. It created an awkward moment that would have been obviated had the court made the inquiry outside the jury's presence. Every criminal defendant has a constitutional right to remain silent, and the exercise of that right should not be a subject for discussion, especially in front of a jury.

I informed the judge that was it was unlikely Mr. Anderson would testify. The judge then raised his gavel, adjourned the day's proceedings, and excused the jury. As he rose from the bench, he indicated a desire to confer with counsel in chambers.

"The defendant will be escorted back to the jail. I would like to speak with counsel in chambers."

As he was being shackled for the shuffle from courtroom to jail, Michael leaned toward me and whispered, "Can the judge force me to testify?"

"Of course not," I answered, reaffirming the bedrock constitutional rule we had talked about on several previous occasions. "I don't know what the judge is up to, Michael, but we'll stop by the jail to talk with you later tonight. We should know more then."

PART 4: DUE PROCESS AND EQUAL PROTECTION

We obediently followed Judge Knight into the borrowed judicial suite that accompanied the borrowed courtroom. I asked the court for permission to smoke. It was 1979.

The judge sat upright in a wooden chair padded in leather with an elongated, curved back panel. It looked like it might be a rocker, but I could not see its legs behind the desk. It didn't matter. Judge Knight was no rocker. Tim and I guessed the judge would want to talk about jury instructions. We thought there was a real chance he might approve of our proposed instructions on lesser included offenses.

Judge Knight's bearing in the privacy of his borrowed office was no less stodgy than his courtroom manner. He started to lecture, "Mr. Critchlow and Mr. Mahoney, you have submitted jury instructions that are significantly different from the prosecutor's instructions. You evidently believe there is a basis to instruct the jury that they can find the defendant guilty of relatively minor offenses instead of the serious felonies with which he is charged. I am not persuaded. To my mind, the testimony is overwhelmingly sufficient to convict your client of kidnapping, robbery, and burglary. There is no evidentiary basis to believe your client is guilty of lesser offenses. The jury will decide if he is guilty or not guilty as charged."

The judge had apparently decided to deny our client his only meaningful and realistic defense before we even had a chance to present a defense. We were disappointed but not shocked. Judge Knight had been an adversary since the beginning. I took a long drag on a Camel cigarette and decided there was nothing to lose by aggressively challenging the court's decision.

"Your honor, I respectfully and emphatically disagree. There is evidence to support the lesser charges, evidence proffered by the prosecution's own witnesses. There is a question about whether the defendant trespassed or committed burglary, a question about the whether he is thief or a robber, and there is uncertainty around whether his restraint of the Carlson family was an unlawful imprisonment or a kidnapping. The jury may or may not agree that the lesser charges are applicable, but the defendant is surely entitled to have his theory of the case put to the jury. If you deny him these instructions, you have denied him the right to a meaningful trial."

Judge Knight rose from his chair. He was positioned between an imposing oak desk and a floor-to-ceiling window that looked out on courthouse grounds. Mature maple trees and blooming yellow tulips bordered lush lawns with signs that warned the riffraff to keep their distance. The judge stood with his back to us and gazed out the window. After a few seconds, he turned sideways and cocked his head in our direction as though he was addressing an invisible audience in front of him but also wanted to make sure people in the cheap seats could hear what he had to say. He was full-bodied, erect, and authoritative.

"Mr. Critchlow, this is not law school, and this is not an intellectual exercise. Everyone in that courtroom knows what your client did, and no one thinks he is guilty of a mere misdemeanor. Now let's get this straight—the man is on trial for serious felonies, and those are the only charges I will allow to be presented to the jury."

"Your honor, I am quite well aware this is not an intellectual exercise. This is the real world and there is no one who knows that better than my client. If he is convicted of the charged felonies, he stands to receive several life sentences. It may very well be that the jury will convict him on these charges. But there is more than a scintilla of evidence in support of our position that the offenses are less serious than charged. The law entitles Mr. Anderson to have a jury decide whether he is guilty of the lesser or greater crimes. He will have a lengthy prison sentence either way but there is a difference between dying in prison and someday being paroled. The prosecution and the court should not dictate the crime when the facts show alternative crimes may have been committed."

Judge Knight appeared to consider my words. I was momentarily hopeful. "Counsel, there is only one way I would grant your request to instruct the jury on the lesser offenses. Mr. Anderson must testify and offer a factual basis to believe that he is something other than a kidnapper, a robber, and a burglar. If he does, I will reconsider."

The prosecutor had sat dispassionately in the corner while the judge and I debated. Now he smiled but said nothing. He knew what Tim and I knew. If we put Anderson on the witness stand, he would be walking into a trap.

I was outraged that the judge would directly try to influence the defendant's constitutionally protected decision to testify or not. I was a young lawyer, but I could recognize blatant judicial overreaching. I knew I had to respond firmly even at the risk of further angering a judge who plainly had no affection for me, my client, or our defense strategy. I needed to do so for the record, for my client, and for the sake of principle. I rose from my chair and stood facing the judge across the desk. He towered above me and a great distance separated us in age, stature, and experience. I didn't care. I vibrated with righteous indignation and partisan passion.

"Judge, with all due respect, I don't believe it is appropriate for the court to pressure the defendant into waiving his right to remain silent," I said. "He should not be faced with the dilemma of having to choose between his Fifth Amendment rights and his entitlement to our proposed jury instructions. In any event, his testimony would simply duplicate and confirm the testimony that has already been presented. What you are proposing is a gift to the prosecutor who would like nothing more than to cross-examine our client. You have departed from your duty to be neutral and impartial."

My sense that Judge Knight was less than fair was validated almost immediately. What happened next was both epic and tragic—epic because it captured and reflected the vestigial underbelly of American history and culture; tragic because that remnant still infected and undermined an American criminal justice system that prided itself on modern principles of constitutional due process and equal protection of the laws.

Judge Knight's face was flushed. Mahoney stood with me, and we faced the judge silently with no intention of throwing fuel on the fire. I had said what needed to be said and was prepared to be rebuked. The judge struggled to compose himself.

"I am going to get that black S.O.B. whether you put him on the stand or not," Judge Knight said. "This discussion is over!"

Chapter 25

"If you are going to say what you want to say, you're going to hear what you don't want to hear."

—Roberto Bolano, *The Insufferable Gaucho*

"Michael, the judge is not exactly warming up to you, us, or our theory of the case," I explained to Anderson when Tim and I met with him that evening in the tiny jailhouse cubicle designated for lawyer visits. "In fact, the judge is out to get you, and said as much. Your race, your color, has something to do with it. I think we should go on the record, call the judge out for being a racist, and seek a mistrial."

"What would that mean?" Michael asked.

Tim's response was clear and emphatic. "Well, he probably won't grant a mistrial, and calling him out will piss him off. If he did grant a mistrial, it means the case would have to be retried with a new judge."

"I don't want to put the Carlson family through this again. It's just not good for anyone. Maybe the prosecutor will just drop the whole thing if we got a mistrial."

"I doubt that very much," Tim said. "The state is bound and determined to take you down."

"How much further down is there? I already have four life terms. Maybe the prosecutors don't care about putting Mrs. Carlson through this again, but I do. I don't want to ask for a mistrial. The judge isn't going to give us one anyway. I want to testify and get this over with."

Tim and I were now extremely wary about putting Michael on the stand. The judge seemed to encourage us to do so, but his angry and bigoted remark revealed a deep animus against our client that made the situation feel impossible. We were not sure how Michael would come across if he did testify, nor could we count on the court to give our jury instructions. The whole thing felt like a set-up. Tim and I believed the judge was, in fact, going to "get" Michael one way or another.

PART 4: DUE PROCESS AND EQUAL PROTECTION

To a criminal defense lawyer in the heat of battle, there is little consolation in knowing the defendant would not be in this position if he had not done some terrible things. In fact, Michael had done terrible things, but an American jury trial puts the system on trial, not just the defendant, and defense lawyers are there to shepherd the process as much as anything. There is a chance for justice when lawyers and judges and jurors see themselves as players whose roles require integrity and good faith even when their private lives are infested with bias and suspicion. The system works, especially for a person of color, only if all the players rise above their idiosyncratic fears and prejudices. In a country that enslaved black people for 250 years, and took another 100 years to outlaw discrimination, hurtful racial attitudes are imbedded in our institutions and can only be eradicated through constant vigilance and effort; the Fourteenth Amendment matters when we act like it matters, when we take its plain language seriously even though its meaning around the edges has been debated for 150 years. An American courtroom is not a special place because of a mystique born of polished wood and emblems and protocols. It is special when people make it so by bringing their better selves.

We did not expect Michael to be found not guilty. We asked only that the jury be given a chance to convict him, on the basis of the evidence, of something less than what the State of Washington charged. To do so, we would need to rely on Judge Knight's good faith.

The conversation with Michael turned to this difficult matter.

"We have advised you against testifying, Michael," I began. "You know that we cannot control what happens when you are cross-examined. However, the judge does not look like he is willing to instruct the jury on lesser offenses unless you testify in a way that supports those instructions. The whole thing stinks."

"I will testify, I will apologize, and I will answer the prosecutor's questions. If it goes bad, so be it. It's not like I have a lot to lose. Someone in the prison could kill me next week, and this whole thing would be a waste of everyone's time."

Michael's testimony would probably not hurt, and could help, so we prepared him the best we could and crossed our fingers. We planned to limit the scope of his testimony as a means of preventing cross-examination on aspects of the case that were unhelpful: the Giant T robbery, putting Ms. Carlson in the trunk of her car, sexual assault, the terrifying trip to Seattle. The general rule of evidence is that an opposing lawyer can only cross-examine a witness on matters to which the witness testified during his direct testimony. The appropriate scope of cross-examination is up to the judge. We warned Michael again about the downside of testifying, but he decided to take the witness stand because he wanted to tell his story in his own words and apologize publicly to the Carlson family.

The next morning, outside the presence of the jury, we informed Judge Knight that the defendant would take the stand to testify about limited issues, including his intentions upon entering the Carlson property, the circumstances surrounding the theft of Mr. Carlson's thirty dollars, and the reasons he tied up the family.

"We have decided Mr. Anderson will testify, your honor," I informed the court. "We would like the court to know in advance that our testimony will be limited in scope and we will oppose any cross-examination outside that scope. Our willingness to testify should not be viewed as a waiver of any right to limit the scope of cross-examination."

Judge Knight looked down from his perch on the bench and a broad smile brightened his face. It was incompatible with his words.

"Thank you, Mr. Critchlow. I must say, I am surprised to hear the defendant will be testifying. It is his right, of course, but I am wondering if your decision to put him on the witness stand is a deliberate effort to set up an appeal issue based on ineffective assistance of counsel. I can't think of another lawyer who would put your client on the stand under these circumstances."

The judge who vowed to "get" our African American client now feigned interest in the quality of our efforts to defend him. The judge who would not consider our jury instructions unless Michael testified now characterized a decision to testify as "ineffective assistance of counsel," the legal phrase describing criminal defense assistance that falls below constitutional standards.

Tim and I were frustrated and indignant but unwilling to turn the trial into a brawl. We had decided not to ask for a mistrial and we were determined to pursue our one and only strategy. Judge Knight would do what he would do.

The judge was not done. Something else bothered him.

"One more thing, counsel, before we bring the jury in. You have both been using the personal pronoun "we" when you should be referring to your client in the third person singular. You are instructed to refer to the defendant as "Mr. Anderson" or "our client." I will not have you confusing this jury by suggesting that you lawyers are somehow identified with the defendant or the outcome of this trial."

* * * *

Michael took the stand and testified in detail about the events related to his entry into the Carlson's home in April of 1978. He spoke in a low voice, barely audible, and his head hung from his shoulders as though he wished to bury his memories. He described his state of mind when he came upon the Carlson home and decided to enter the open back door to seek refuge from the cold and rain. He was running from the police but not looking to hurt anyone. He had no desire to contact the family or steal their possessions. He confessed to what might be described as an illegal entry, a misdemeanor. Michael then talked about his decision to tie up the family members in order to keep them restrained and quiet while he decided what to do. He admitted to facts that arguably constituted unlawful imprisonment rather than kidnapping under Washington law. Finally, Michael testified about taking thirty dollars from Mr. Carlson's wallet before he left the house with Mrs. Carlson. The wallet lay on a table and there was no struggle or threat of violence connected to Michael's appropriation of the funds. In his mind, he had committed petty theft.

Michael was about finished. He lifted his eyes and looked at the jury.

"I have only one more thing to say. I want to apologize to every member of the Carlson family for what I put them through. It was wrong and I am sorry. I especially want to apologize to Mrs. Carlson. I never intended to hurt her when I entered the house. I just panicked when she discovered me, and I lost control. I am ashamed of hurting this woman and I wish I could take it back."

His direct testimony was concluded. It provided a foundation for instructing the jury on offenses that would yield something less than life sentences if Michael was found guilty. This was Michael's case, in a nutshell, and his only hope for someday walking out of prison.

The prosecutor started in on him. The cross-examination was thorough, systematic, and brutal. It also went far beyond the scope of Michael's direct examination and the judge allowed it over Tim's and my vociferous objections. Michael had carefully avoided any mention of the events that happened in Benton County, the dash across the state, or the culminating events in Seattle.

The prosecutor first spent a good deal of time patiently asking Michael to affirm his previous criminal convictions dating back to his early adult life in Illinois. The jury heard about attempted murder, assaults, robberies, and carjacking. They were told about Michael's time at the Illinois State Penitentiary in Joliet. The prosecutor artfully followed that line of inquiry by having Michael describe his current residence at the Washington State Penitentiary. And then:

"And why are you at the Washington Penitentiary, Mr. Anderson? Is it because you were convicted of robbery and kidnapping in Benton County?"

Finally, after exhaustively exploring Michael's criminal history, the prosecutor inquired about the jail escape and Michael's desperate attempt to flee Pasco and the police.

"You would do just about anything or hurt just about anyone in order to get away, wouldn't you, Mr. Anderson?"

The cross-examination was as expected, but the prosecutor had prepared one last question as his finale.

"You say you did not want to hurt Mrs. Carlson, is that correct Mr. Anderson? Is that why you raped her and locked her in a car trunk?"

These matters were far beyond the scope of what Michael had testified to on direct examination. We believed the questions were improper and deliberately planned so that the jury would hear the substance of the charge before we had time to object. We did object loudly and aggressively. The judge excused the jury and took a recess. He called us into chambers and smugly lectured about the dangers of having our client testify and opening up the door to cross-examination on matters that were not otherwise in evidence.

"Counsel, you opened the door when you decided, against my advice, to put your client on the stand. Your client opened the door when he testified about not wanting to hurt Mrs. Carlson. The prosecutor merely walked through that open door. Live and learn, counsel. Now, let's finish this trial!"

The prosecutor finished his cross-examination. I knew Michael's apology and concerns for the well-being of Mrs. Carlson were heartfelt, but the disclosures elicited on cross-examination underscored for the jury that the defendant was a very dangerous man indeed.

We finished the trial with a couple of witnesses who fleshed out Michael's personality and character in the context of the time he had spent in the Franklin County Jail. It was time to finalize jury instructions and, to that end, the judge called us into chambers.

PART 4: DUE PROCESS AND EQUAL PROTECTION

It did not take long to appreciate how far the judge had led us down the primrose path. Judge Knight did not sit, did not offer us a beverage, and did not invite small talk. I resisted the temptation to light a Camel.

"Gentlemen, the evidence supports the charges filed against the defendant by the prosecutor's office. It does not support the alternative crimes proposed by the defendant. I will instruct the jury with our stock instructions, including the enumerated offenses of burglary, kidnapping, and robbery. Counsel for the defense can make any objections they like on the record. We will instruct the jury tomorrow morning followed immediately by closing arguments. You all have a nice evening."

* * * *

The last day of trial was the kind of warm summer day that makes you want to lay on your back and watch the sun peek through gigantic cumulus clouds. Independence Day was around the corner, nearby lakes beckoned, and jurors missed their families. Everyone wanted the trial to end, but there was work to be done and jurors seemed determined to take their duty seriously. They were alert and engaged as they listened to Judge Knight's lengthy legal instructions before hearing final arguments and deliberating a verdict.

The court instructed the jury in accordance with the prosecutor's wishes. The jury could convict Anderson, or not, of kidnapping, burglary, and robbery. Lesser charges were not on the table. Tim Mahoney and I gave closing arguments intended to focus the jurors' attention on small factual discrepancies and legal definitions that raised questions as to whether or not the prosecution had proved all charges beyond a reasonable doubt. In the absence of our proposed instructions on lesser offenses, we did not expect a good result.

The jury retired to deliberate at 11:46 AM. Michael was returned to the county jail, and Tim and I withdrew to an air-conditioned local tavern where we ordered burgers, sipped beer, and conducted the inevitable postmortem. The trial had not gone as we had hoped, but we had given it our best shot, and given Michael his day in court.

To our surprise, the jury deliberated for hours. We had apparently succeeded in giving them something to think about. In the end, it was wishful thinking. The jury delivered its verdict at 5:12 later that afternoon. Michael was found guilty of four counts of first-degree kidnapping and one count of armed robbery. We had won on the burglary charge only. The jury had apparently agreed that Michael was a trespasser, but not a burglar, when he first entered the Carlson house.

Formal sentencing was scheduled for some time in September 1979. Corrections officials would have plenty of time to prepare and present information and recommendations relating to Anderson's life, criminal history, and prospects for rehabilitation.

In the meantime, there were more charges to adjudicate.

* * * *

A month later, we returned to Spokane to try the remaining Franklin County criminal charges against Anderson. This was the bifurcated trial involving charges unrelated to the Carlson home invasion. A different judge, Judge Parsons, presided. The case was a "who done it" inquiry involving questionable witness identification, law enforcement bias, and alibi evidence. The verdict of the all-white jury after a week of trial produced mixed results. Michael was acquitted on six felony charges and convicted of three—two armed robberies and an assault.

In the end, the two trials resulted in Michael's conviction on nine of the original twenty-two counts with which he was charged in Franklin County. His successful defense on thirteen alleged felonies meant that someday a parole board would have thirteen fewer reasons to keep him in prison. At the time, this was hardly something to celebrate. Although Michael had not yet been sentenced, I knew he would likely spend his life in prison. I derived nothing more than fleeting pleasure from the acquittals.

Part 5: The Great Mandala (Wheel of Life)

Chapter 26

"We all die. The goal isn't to live forever, the goal is to create something that will."

—Chuck Palahniuk

I left my father's law firm in January 1980 after three years of private practice, and not long after the Michael Anderson case was finished. My name was on the firm door, and it would have been reasonable and lucrative for me to spend the rest of my professional life there. However, I had a hunch that I belonged somewhere else. I received a serendipitous call from a former law school teacher advising me of a new law school faculty position that needed to be filled in the school's clinical program. Might I be interested? I was. There was no promise of job security beyond a one-year contract. Still, it was the kind of timely opportunity that mysteriously presents itself when the requisite forces are in alignment. I applied for and was offered the job—a job that today would almost certainly be filled only after an intensive national search for a candidate whose credentials and experience far exceeded what I possessed in 1980. I am often asked how I became a law school professor, and I respond by telling people I snuck in the back door.

So, it happened that I returned to Gonzaga University School of Law in Spokane, the same law school I had attended as a student. I was grateful to my father and his partners for hiring me and introducing me to the exciting world of litigation. They had trained me and enabled me to have professional opportunities and a measure of success not easily achieved by young lawyers. There was some guilt around the fact that the firm had invested in my training and mentorship and would not now reap the financial rewards that ordinarily flow from such an investment. My dad was uncomplaining though. He understood that the world was big and inviting, and it was important for me to untether my life from his law firm. He had made deep tracks in the local legal landscape, and it was time for me to make my own tracks elsewhere. Dad was sincere in wishing me the best and he helped make the transition smooth and easy.

There was an appealing stucco-style apartment complex on Spokane's lower South Hill that I had admired since my law school days. It had, on two levels, a couple of bedrooms, a bathroom, kitchen, and living room. It was all brick with a quiet courtyard, trees, and a bit of lawn. The doors and window frames were arched, the floors all tile and oak, and the overall ambience almost Moorish. There was a vacancy and I moved in. I had a television, a stereo, my clothes, and not much more. The new life I had chosen would be up and down, like all lives, and I would sometimes second-guess my decision to leave the comfort and predictability of my father's law firm. I knew my move to Spokane did not place me on the path to getting rich, but I was happy and looking forward to the challenge of being a teacher as well as a lawyer.

Dad visited me occasionally during the first several months after I moved to Spokane. By that time, he had been divorced for four years from my mother and was romantically involved with a woman in Spokane. He introduced me to the woman, Carolee, and I immediately liked her. She was both the girl next door and a little exotic. She enjoyed books, classical music, and metaphysics while juggling the activities and demands of mostly grown children. Her comfortable three-story home in an old and fashionable South Hill neighborhood was filled with soft things and overstuffed chairs. The memorabilia and furnishings revealed rich and varied interests in travel, art, and matters of the spirit. I believed the woman's influence and company would be emotionally stabilizing and intellectually stimulating for an aging lawyer like my father who was finally exploring life beyond work and a failed marriage.

Dad, Carolee, and I met for drinks and meals several times in the winter and spring of 1980. Then came the volcano. Mount St. Helen's had been visibly simmering for months before it finally exploded on May 18, 1980, with the force of 1,600 atomic bombs of the type that destroyed Hiroshima.

No one really expects to witness the historic spectacle of a major North American mountain blowing its top. Dad was in Richland when the mountain erupted. Michael was at the penitentiary in Walla Walla. They

PART 5: THE GREAT MANDALA (WHEEL OF LIFE)

both caught only a peripheral bit of the massive cloud of smoke and ash that turned central and northeastern Washington's day into night. I experienced its full force. From the top of a friend's home where I was enjoying a Sunday morning brunch, I watched the horizon gradually darken and then blacken as the volcano's ash began to rain down on Spokane and the surrounding region in eerie silence. It was like a heavy winter snowstorm—except that everything was covered by thick blankets of gray and gritty dust. After a day or so, when it was finally over, several inches of ash covered the city, creating a transportation and respiratory emergency that kept people in their homes for days. The clean-up took weeks. The ash was plowed like snow into heaps along the sides of roads. It had followed the path of the prevailing wind and was part of the landscape of northeastern Washington, northern Idaho, and western Montana for many years to come.

I last saw my dad at a downtown Spokane restaurant and jazz bar in June. Dad wanted to see Carolee and also the volcano's effects. It was a cool summer evening, and he looked fit and healthy in a dark-blue V-neck sweater with a button-down light-blue dress shirt and khaki pants. His face, framed by his still thick and abundant white hair, was tanned and chiseled. At sixty-two, the years had sculpted him without diminishing his good looks or personality. We talked, sipped Scotch, and listened to music. I was becoming increasingly comfortable around Carolee, and I hoped her relationship with dad had legs. I was pleased when they told me they would be spending a week together the next month backpacking with an Episcopal church group in the North Cascade mountains. As I rose to leave, Dad would not let me pay any part of the bill. He asked if there was anything I needed. I said I was fine. We shook hands and said goodbye.

As I turned to go, Dad spoke the last words I ever heard him say: "If you should ever want to make some extra money, I could send you a client or two."

Occasionally I had unfinished legal business for clients in Benton County and would need to make the three-hour drive from Spokane to the courthouse in Prosser. It was a July day in 1980 when Judge Yencopal called me into his judicial chambers much the same way he had beckoned me at the time he assigned me the task of representing Michael Anderson. The judge did not invite me to his office for small talk.

"I have bad news, George," the judge began. "Your father died this morning in a backpacking accident in the mountains above Lake Chelan. I don't know any details. His office in Richland was notified. They knew you would be here today, so they called and asked me to deliver the news. I am very sorry and very sad. Your father was a good man, and I loved him."

I had experienced the death of grandparents and a few acquaintances, but I had never encountered the sudden, unexpected death of a close family member, certainly not a parent. It comes like a sucker punch to the head, knocks you back, unbalances you, and instantly changes your perception of all things that comprise your former life. People, priorities, the physical world, and time itself start bending in a way that distorts your sense of reality. You discover that particles are, indeed, waves. Thoughts are interchangeable with feelings, and you are unanchored and floating. You are wrapped in a surreal fog and you reach, in vain, to touch the living presence of one whose evanescence is dreamlike. In time, after bereavement and tears, after the celebration of life and memories that allows us to finally accept a loved one's death, we are restored to normalcy, but it is a new normalcy because we have lost a parent and must reimagine our lives and accept the certainty of our own passing.

* * * *

And so, I began a new phase of my life teaching students how to be lawyers. I mostly taught the skills associated with representing clients and resolving disputes. I also taught traditional classes—civil procedure, criminal procedure, and professional responsibility—but most of my career has been clinically oriented, meaning that I supervised students one-on-one in a law school "clinic" where students represented actual clients. In addition to teaching, law school faculty are expected to handle some administrative responsibilities and participate in the governance of the law school through committee work and faculty meetings. Committees managed curriculum issues and contributed to admissions work, budgeting, and recruitment and retention of new faculty. I did my share of this work and gradually became familiar with most aspects of law school operations and governance. I worked under several deans and formed opinions about what personal qualities and leadership styles were most valuable.

When I was young, I never expected to be a lawyer. I have touched on the conflict I felt when first starting law school. When I was a young clinical teacher working on a year-to-year contract, I lived a life of teaching students how to handle garden-variety divorces, draft wills, and try drunk driving cases. It was not my intention to grow into a traditional academic who wrote scholarly articles and debated esoteric points of law and pedagogy. I also did not plan to compete for an appointment of lifetime tenure. When that tenure was conferred, I never once imagined myself as dean of the law school. I didn't suppose anyone else visualized me in that role either. So, when a colleague approached me to talk about submitting my name as a candidate for an interim dean position, it was unexpected and uninvited. But the law school needed a steady, guiding hand at the time, and the job would be temporary, so I agreed to think about it.

Chapter 27

*"A great marriage is not when the 'perfect couple' come together.
It is when an imperfect couple learns to enjoy their differences."*

—Dave Meur

While Michael experienced a profound spiritual metamorphosis, I pursued one more of many romantic relationships. Diane and I started dating in Spokane in 1992. I left her to go to Romania shortly afterward. I had received a Fulbright Fellowship that extended for a full year and, given the distance, I did not want to promise or talk of commitment. But we communicated by letter and phone and our relationship deepened until I invited her to meet me in London, where we decided to get engaged. I bowed to convention, somewhat reluctantly, and we shopped for a ring in London's famed diamond district, a day-long ordeal I hope never to repeat. My advice to anyone looking to buy an engagement ring is decidedly unromantic but practical: give a generous sum of money to your beloved and trust his or her judgment in selecting fine jewelry.

The engagement stuck—perhaps because Diane tolerated my idiosyncratic, aging obduracy. She returned to her life in Beverly Hills, where she lived in a condominium not far from Rodeo Drive. At the University of Sibiu, in Transylvania, I was living in a tiny room with a fussy gas heater that had exploded and no longer worked. There was a dated black-and-white, Russian-made television and a bathroom down the hall with no hot water, shower, or heat. I had a few months off for summer break. I looked around and decided to fly to Beverly Hills.

The train ride from Sibiu to Bucharest took six hours and was very hot. Like most Romanian trains of the time, it was quite old and had no water or functional bathroom. No matter, because I had arranged to spend the night in an upscale Bucharest hotel before flying out the next morning. Bucharest was also hot. Hot and septic. Untreated blue-gray exhaust poured from buses and cars and fouled the city's air. A taxi dropped me at the hotel, and I checked in—excited about the prospect of a shave and shower. I could not take a proper shower in Sibiu, so a shower in this nice hotel, especially after a long, grimy train trip, would be heaven. I had booked an early morning flight from Bucharest to Chicago and on to Los Angeles. There would be long hours of travel, but at least I would be clean, shaved, and well-rested.

My room was on an upper floor. It was well-appointed and looked rather Byzantine in keeping with the Turks' historic influence in the Balkans. I quickly made my way to the bathroom and turned on the shower's hot water. There was no response, not a drop of water dribbled from the ornamental shower fitting. I tried the cold water. Nothing. I whirled around to the bathroom sink. Still nothing. *Well, maybe this is a problem unique to this room. I'll ask for another room.* I called the receptionist and reported the problem, reminding her that, when I booked the room, the hotel had said it had water. The receptionist was very polite and respectful as she explained, in perfect English, that the hotel did have water. Unfortunately, due to municipal water policy, it was only available four days a week, and this was not one of those days.

This was the city of Bucharest after forty-five years of stifling and tyrannical government clumsiness. This was the city of Bucharest that could not supply residents with water but boasted the second largest governmental building in the world, the "People's House," comprised of 1,100 marble inlaid rooms, built by the former dictator Nicolae Ceausescu to memorialize his own eminence and vision of a socialist world that resembled the hierarchy in George Orwell's *Animal Farm,* where "all animals are equal but some animals are more equal than others." We can safely assume that Nicolae Ceausescu never went a day without water.

The hotel also lacked air conditioning. I slept fitfully in the heat. I arose early feeling dirty and grumpy. Bottled water supplied by the hotel enabled me to brush my teeth and splash water on my face. The taxi driver doubled the normal price of my ride to the airport. When I protested, he argued that I was obliged to pay for his way back into the city because it was unlikely he could corral a return fare at that time of morning. I relented. The plane was delayed, and I wandered the gloomy corridors of the old airport inspecting the beat-up planes flown by TAROM, the Romanian national airline. When my flight was ready, I was confused because there were no passengers at the designated gate. The attendant confirmed I was in the right place, took my ticket, and ushered me onto what appeared to be a first-generation Boeing 707 airliner dating back, perhaps, to the 1950s. There were three other passengers, besides me, and a crew of seven or eight attractive Romanian flight attendants. It was a long flight to Chicago. I was tired and unwashed. But I did not remain cranky for long, surrounded as I was by an entourage of lovely, sable-haired women whose job was to keep me comfortable on a big empty jet headed west to the land of hot showers and catalytic converters.

Diane picked me up at LAX, and we drove straight to Beverly Hills, a short trip that underscored at every turn the extraordinary contrast between a luxurious existence in one of America's most affluent communities and the Romanian struggle for subsistence in one of Eastern Europe's poorest countries. Diane amused herself in the posh lifestyle of the Beverly Hills elite. She was living temporarily with her niece, a model and aspiring actress. In a previous life, Diane had helped build a church in an impoverished urban community in New Jersey. Oddly, during that same period, she also toured the country as a vocalist for a rock band and worked as a fit model for Liz Claiborne in Manhattan. Diane tolerated Beverly Hills' excesses but was not seduced by its values or dreamy veneer. She was basically marking time until my Romanian adventure concluded, and we could plan our marriage and get on with our lives. Over the next two decades, Diane would tour the country and world as a representative of a youth travel program, obtain a master's degree in counseling, direct a residential program for disadvantaged and homeless women, and supervise practicum programs for Gonzaga University's School of Education. However, becoming a mother and raising our daughter, Charlotte, was easily her most fulfilling role.

I played some golf, went to the beach, saw a few celebrities, and enjoyed evenings of fine dining and drinks at swanky restaurants that cost more than the monthly stipends I received as a Fulbright professor teaching in Romania. One day, as I wandered the aisles of a Beverly Hills Whole Foods store, I ran into my high school girlfriend who I had not seen for twenty-five years. The next night, Diane and I dined at a restaurant on Rodeo Drive and were stunned to find the same old girlfriend and her husband, a Beverly Hills psychiatrist, seated next to us. The husband shook my hand and said something about how delightfully serendipitous it was for his wife to keep running into me.

This was all a little surreal. Part of me was occupied by my life and ongoing responsibilities in Romania, and it was hard for me to reconcile that endeavor with window shopping on Rodeo Drive. After a few weeks in Beverly Hills, I was done. Diane was also ready to get out of La-La Land, so we crammed her belongings and my suitcase into her 1975 Volvo, the "Orange

PART 5: THE GREAT MANDALA (WHEEL OF LIFE)

Pumpkin," extended our best wishes to her niece, and drove north to Spokane. We were undecided if Diane would join me when I returned to Sibiu. I left her to think about it and joined friends on a ten-day kayaking trip in Glacier Bay, Alaska. I was continuing to live as though I was single, a pattern that was in tension with our engagement and the need to focus on making a life together. When I returned from Alaska with stories about calving glaciers and the aurora borealis, Diane wondered aloud if there was room for her in my self-centered universe. We talked and agreed that we would put our relationship to the test by living together in a ravaged economy in a distant land where fruits and vegetables were hard to come by, donkeys and sheep shared the streets, and a hot shower was a luxury.

So, Diane joined me in Transylvania for the fall, and we spent several satisfying months focused on each other, on friends and students, and the challenges of an emerging economy and rapidly changing culture. Diane was a veritable trooper, waiting in line every day to buy bread and cheese, sorting through remnants of the summer's harvest at the local street market to find a few good vegetables, washing clothes by hand in the sink, and embracing the Romanian people's capacity to endure water shortages, electrical outages, and empty shelves. We were away from the allure of movies, television, malls, restaurants, freeways, fast cars, and technology. Our lives slowed. We walked everywhere. We had long dinners with friends and drank excellent local wine that cost a dollar a bottle. Diane donated time at a local orphanage where needy children, many disabled, clutched at her like babies begging for an absent mother. I taught human rights and comparative law to students starved for information in an education culture crippled by generations of centralized control, censorship, and fear. We bought a butchered turkey in Bucharest, packed it in ice for the six-hour train ride back to Sibiu, and pulled together random scraps of food to serve an American-style Thanksgiving dinner to several American students attending the University of Sibiu on an exchange program.

One stormy night, we watched *Bram Stoker's Dracula* on a big television screen at the home of a friend who worked in the German Consulate. We walked home through shadowy streets filled with wind-blown leaves under a fittingly full Transylvanian moon. We attended classical concerts and choral performances in old and beautiful Romanian Orthodox churches decorated with hand-painted icons and frescoes dating back to medieval times. I became enamored of the nineteenth-century Romantic poet, Mihai Eminescu, and learned something of the rich folk tradition and mythology that inform the Orthodox Church's religious beliefs and art. Romania has romantic and mystical dimensions that require time and patience to appreciate. We were there long enough to feel a bit of the enduring soul that fortifies a long-suffering people.

> *All things that exist today*
> *Suffer the same destiny,*
> *Different masks, but same play,*
> *Other lips, same harmony*
> *And for thousands of centuries*
> *We've laughed or shed a tear;*
> *So, you, deluded down the ages,*
> *Have no hope and have no fear.*
>
> —MIHAI EMINESCU, "GLOSS"

Another few years would pass before Diane and I escaped to Banff, Alberta to exchange simple wedding vows in the presence of a holy woman, our dogs, and a couple of friends. But it was that time together in Transylvania that made it possible. My year in Romania helped me in my long journey toward reconciliation of the part of me that wanted to be distant and alone and the part that craved intimacy. The experience also enhanced my understanding of how truly privileged many of us are. I would never again be able to listen to people of wealth and position talk about minor annoyances without saying to myself, or out loud, "First world problem."

Chapter 28

*"Where, after all, do universal human rights begin?
In small places close to home...."*

—Eleanor Roosevelt

I was proud to be a lawyer and professor involved in providing access to justice for poor people. But for many years my days and nights were suffused with anxiety and guilt. I was not as productive, prepared, disciplined, generous, sensitive, understanding, effective, and multitalented as I thought I should be. Some suspicion of inadequacy always lay submerged below my confident professional veneer. I should have returned that phone call; I shouldn't have been so adversarial with opposing counsel; I should read more law review articles in preparing to teach a class; I should be more empathetic with students and clients; I should work this weekend to get caught up; I should learn French, volunteer for more boards or committees, be nicer to support staff; and, for sure, I should figure out how to research investment opportunities so my wife and I don't go on welfare when they find out I really am inadequate and I lose my job.

Other lawyers may know this feeling. Over time we come to believe that what we do professionally, socially, and economically are the only things that count. We are driven and haunted by the knowledge that there is always something more we could be doing. We work hard. We problem solve. We keep up with the pace of cultural change. We are proactive. The notion of doing nothing may seem nice in some abstract, utopian, Buddhist sort of way—but, really, it's subversive to how we define ourselves. Thanks to digital technology, 24/7 news, espresso bars, political scandal, fast food, junk TV, thrill-seeking, endless clients, controversies, famous people, and volatile stock funds, we are constantly engaged, moving forward, afraid we will fall behind.

Billy, the diminutive character of conscience played by Linda Hunt in the film *The Year of Living Dangerously*, observes: "We make a fetish of our careers. All else becomes secondary. Where is there space for us to learn to love?"

This all changed for me at age fifty. One morning in early 2001, I lay the beautiful, perfect, eleven-month-old Charlotte Isabella on her changing pad on the floor, stripped off her diapers, and was relieved to find no smelly mess. I left the room for a moment leaving Charlotte unattended but content. When I returned, she had crawled off the changing pad, onto the expensive, imported Chinese carpet, and delivered herself of the well-digested residue of several recent meals. The stuff was all over baby and carpet.

After my wife and I returned from China in December 2000 with our newly adopted first child, every day presented an opportunity for me to learn something new. I learned to appreciate quiet time and naps, gentle touches, and leak-proof diapers. And dancing. On the Saturday morning of Charlotte's untimely mess, after the cleanup and bath, the apples and mango breakfast, the walk in the snow with the dogs, Charlotte and I danced to Bob Dylan, Toni Braxton, Miles Davis, and a recent release by Eric Clapton and B. B. King. She loved it all, but the Clapton-King collaboration was her favorite. I loved it all too. Not for a moment did I feel guilty or anxious about neglecting my career or the rest of the world. If I felt inadequate at all, it had to do with not understanding how an imperfect guy could be blessed with such a perfect little treasure.

The experience did not last, and I gradually returned to the habits of a demanding and neurotic professional life. Still, there is an unbroken thread that connects the wonder and responsibility of having a baby and the work we do as lawyers. Lawyers can be shepherds of justice and human rights. There was a colorful illustration that hung on my office wall for many years depicting mother and child and the inspiring words of Eleanor Roosevelt. I did not fully apprehend their truth until Charlotte came into our lives:

Where, after all,
do universal human rights begin?
In small places close to home—
so close and so small
that they cannot be seen on
any maps of the world . . .
Unless these rights have meaning there,
they have little meaning anywhere.

PART 5: THE GREAT MANDALA (WHEEL OF LIFE)

When Charlotte was about four or five years old, we vacationed on the northern Oregon coast at Gearhart, a charming little village with classic, gray-shingled beach houses and a large hotel complemented by the oldest golf course in Oregon, the Gearhart Golf Links, a misty, windswept field of green with lots of shrub conifers bent permanently by the west wind. Gearhart is about an hour's drive west of Portland. Like so many inviting towns on the Oregon coast, it is expensive and white. Charlotte, my wife, and I were eating dinner and chatting one night at a beachside restaurant. I don't remember what we were talking about, or whether we were talking at all. Completely out of the blue, Charlotte spoke up and asked, "What's the deal with all the white people?" I paused, took a sip of wine, and looked at Diane. She smiled and nodded in my direction, indicating that I should take a crack at answering the question.

"Well, honey," I began, "there are lots of people in the world. A long time ago, they all came from a place where everyone looked the same. Later, they became people of different colors depending on where they lived. Black people came mostly from a place called Africa. American Indians came from right here, in our country, America. White people came from across the ocean in Europe. There were more white people who came here than anyone else. That's why you see so many of them."

I paused, and Charlotte just stared at me . . . . waiting.

"And you, Boopsy, came from China, a big country where many, many people have beautiful skin like yours. Someday we will visit China and you will know what it's like to be around people who look like you."

Charlotte nodded, said "Okay," and didn't mention the subject again for many years. When she did, we were in Guangzhou, China visiting the orphanage where Charlotte had spent the first ten months of her life. She was seventeen, sophisticated, well-traveled, smart, and all-American. She asked the orphanage director if China would ever have a DNA database that might enable her to determine if she had a biological sibling. The director replied that such a thing might be possible in the next twenty years. As we left Guangzhou, Charlotte said, "Dad, it is so nice to be around people who look like me."

Chapter 29

"I remember her... on long drives
and endless highways..."

My life and Michael's overlapped in unpredictable and serendipitous ways. Dee and Michael had moved to Pasco in 1977 because Dee had cousins there—the Kinsey family. My sister, Ann—the one who many years before sat in an unwelcoming Selma, Alabama, restaurant with Gramps, me, and her black friend—had a long-term, off-and-on-again relationship with one of these cousins, Steve Kinsey. Steve was a sweet man who had suffered from years of drug addiction and periodic incarceration. Ann and Steve were both troubled, but they gave one another something they could not find elsewhere.

Ann lived an unusual, jumbled life that stretched from five years in an Episcopal boarding school in Walla Walla to civil rights work in 1960s rural Alabama and laboring as a Teamster on Seattle's waterfront, to employment as a paralegal, alcohol counselor, and probation officer. In between, there was a degree in African American studies at the University of Washington, a posse of unconventional friends, obsession with crime and the criminal justice system, alcoholism, and a private interior drama that rivaled anything that might transpire in the world of shared, observable experience. My sister inherited my parents' and grandparents' political sensibilities, especially around issues of racial justice, and this produced idealism that was in constant war with her lived experience.

Ann's life ended at age fifty-seven, in 2005, when she could no longer endure the daily struggle to reconcile reality and delusion. She suffered from a bipolar condition, or mild schizophrenia, or some combination of the two, depending on what the psychiatric specialists might say on a given day or year. People afflicted with these conditions typically show symptoms by early adulthood. Less frequently, the mental health issues appear later in life, as was the case with my sister.

PART 5: THE GREAT MANDALA (WHEEL OF LIFE)

My mother knew Ann had problems but figured they could be overcome by changing her hairdo and getting a nice, colorful dress. That could lead to meeting a nice young man, dating, marriage, and a happy and stable life. But Ann's hair was often long and untamed, and she would sometimes hide behind her thick mane and drive Mom crazy. At other times, her hair was big and round and frizzy in an Afro style that mirrored her poodle, Krypto, and betrayed her affection for the look and feel of black culture. Mom, of course, knew the truth about Ann's mental health issues and quietly lived with both the pain of that truth and the self-reproach that is the inevitable burden of being a parent of a hurting child.

Mom always hoped to mitigate Ann's stress and one Christmas, when Ann was about fifty years old, my mom bought her a vibrator, thinking it was an electronic massaging device for the neck and shoulders. Mom's life was not always traditional, but in matters of sex, it is safe to say her experience was limited. Our custom as a family was to unwrap Christmas gifts one by one in rotation. It was Ann's turn, and we all watched expectantly.

Ann pulled the vibrator out of the box, read the card from my mom, smirked, and coolly asked, "Mom, exactly what is it that you would like me to do with this?"

Without batting an eye, mom reached over and took the vibrator. She switched it to on and calmly started massaging her own neck and shoulders with the business end of the gadget. "You see," she said, "this is a wonderful way for you to relax those parts of your body that are hard to get at. I think you'll really enjoy it."

The extended family of five siblings, in-laws, and grandchildren watched all this unfold. There was initial confusion, then astonishment as people recognized the gift for what it was and exchanged knowing looks. No one said a word, in deference to Mom, and we all tried mightily to suppress laughter that really, under the circumstances, no one could be expected to contain, and it all finally busted out in great waves of howling hilarity. My poor mom didn't get it, until later when one of my sisters took her aside to explain. Ann enjoyed telling the story for years afterwards, her amusement heightened, I think, by the fact that, for once, it was Mom who was seen as the peculiar one.

Ann's way of being in the world germinated in an emerging baby boom culture. However, she was never a slave to that culture's trends or looks or attitudes. She was white but often felt more comfortable around her African American friends. She was hip, but not a hippie, compassionate but brutally honest, and prickly about being told what to do. She opposed drug use but dated drug users. Her early instincts were to engage the world and work for social justice. That gradually gave way to a more inactive, cloistered life that allowed her to retreat into the interior narratives that increasingly dominated her mental life. Ann swam competitively as a child, but that experience may have drained her of any further interest in physical activity. She was a homebody who preferred her cats and couch to a walk in the park.

Toward the end, Ann lived for some years in Kalispell, Montana, not far from my sister Mary. Mary kept an eye on Ann, as did my mother who lived in nearby Big Fork, Montana, at the time. Then Ann moved to Spokane and experienced a gradual decline in her mental health. She made me crazy, but I loved her and looked after her as best I could—made sure she got her disability checks, her food stamps, and stayed in touch with assigned mental health professionals. She subsisted on carbohydrates and Coca-Cola, smoked, and sat, often with a thin, knowing smile, or an unintelligible comment that confirmed she had withdrawn into an internal discourse that was inaccessible to others. Occasionally she would struggle to communicate to me the actual content of this interior world—the demons and disorder and danger, danger not just to the imaginary players that populated Ann's troubled mind, but dangers she feared would be visited upon real world actors—family and friends and certain government officials.

She occasionally threatened or attempted suicide, to which I typically responded by having her involuntarily committed for short periods of time. On one such occasion, sometime in the early years of the new millennium, she invoked her due process right to a commitment hearing before a local judge. I was called as a witness by a veteran mental health court prosecutor, who accurately believed Ann was a threat to herself if allowed back into the community. The hearing took place at the end of a long hallway in a shabbily furnished room located among institutional administrative offices in an aging brownstone mental health hospital. Ann understood I was acting in good faith and that I had well-founded concerns about her mental stability and suicidal propensities. Still, she could not resist the judge's invitation to cross-examine me, and she did so in a manner that exposed her quick wit and ironic sense of humor even in the midst of a serious inquiry into matters of existential consequence.

"So, you are my brother, correct?" she began.

"Yes," I answered.

PART 5: THE GREAT MANDALA (WHEEL OF LIFE)

"And, it is your testimony that you have my best interests in mind, is that correct?"

"Yes."

"And you have told me previously, haven't you, that as my brother, you will not sit by and let me make my own decision about dying?"

"Yes, I believe I have said something along those lines," I responded, not quite knowing what Ann was getting at.

"So, your mind is made up regardless of the quality of my life or how miserable I am?"

I could now sense the logic behind this line of questioning, and it worried me that Ann could conduct such a focused and rational cross-examination in the face of my earlier testimony that she was acting irrationally. What might the judge be thinking?

I answered the question. "I suppose my mind is fixed, yes. I love you. You are my sister. And I will do everything I can to prevent you from hurting yourself."

Ann concluded her cross-examination. "Thank you. I believe I have made my point—two points actually. First, your relationship to me as a sibling creates a conflict of interest. Second, you are close-minded."

When dealing with mental illness, there is always the thought that you can change an afflicted person's thinking by persuading with logic and facts. It is hard to finally let that go, hard because we fear for our own sanity when we surrender logic to craziness, and because we hope the craziness, in any event, is simply an annoying and anomalous lesion that, when treated, will permit a return to good health and normal behavior. I did let it go, finally, on the occasion when I found thousands of Ann's anti-psychotic meds squirreled away in grocery bags in the corner of her closet. Why she did not simply throw them in the garbage or flush them down the toilet, I don't know. I do know she kept refilling her unused prescriptions because she did not want to upset her assigned mental health professionals or put her government benefits at risk. When I confronted her about the meds, she frankly explained that she preferred struggling with her demons to feeling numb. Letting go, for me, did not help Ann get better but it helped me be less anxious and more able to be with her as a brother and friend instead of an adversary.

I was not surprised when Ann finally succeeded in killing herself. After unsuccessful earlier attempts, she announced emphatically that she would do so again. The death itself was unremarkable, a cold body in a dark room surrounded by pill bottles, no death note, and two cats in the yard. Life used to be so hard, but this was an end to Ann's nightmare and, for my siblings and me, a sad and resigned occasion to celebrate a life that fit no mold and was not accountable to convention. There is something to be said for living an authentic life and Ann's was lived without apology. She was dry, honest, sometimes sentimental, sometimes not, and bereft of guile. When she was on, she had laser-focused interpersonal skills. She made others feel comfortable and worthy because, like my mother, she communicated genuine interest in their lives and feelings. She lived in the realm of feelings and could ferret out the emotional story behind the events—mundane or momentous—that shaped the lives of those close to her.

Ann was troubled, yes, but always fully human. I remember her, especially on long drives and endless highways, in places like Montana, where a body can get lost, and the sky is big and welcoming and forgiving.

Part 6: Empathy and Faith

Chapter 30

"The more you learn about someone, how could you not want to protect them and their rights? The more you learn about a culture or a certain identity, it's hard to not feel empathy."

—Yara Shahidi

What is empathy and what role does it play in our lives? What should we make of a man like Michael Anderson who spent a good chunk of his young life hurting people? What is there to say about a judge who says of a party before the court: "I am going to get that black S.O.B."? How do we interpret our own behavior when we discount other peoples' feelings, marginalize people who are different, and substitute aggression for conciliation? My view is that these are all variations on the human tendency to dehumanize people who are different in look, lifestyle, religion, or ideas. This tendency is so pervasive and so evident throughout history and cultures, that it is tempting to explain it biologically. Are we simply hardwired to fear the other? Are we *by nature* likely to question another person's value simply because he or she is not part of our family or tribe? Does difference trigger evolutionary responses that were once necessary to protect us against outsiders? If so, it seems to me the modern antidote to atavistic fear is empathy.

Psychologists agree that empathy is a key ingredient of successful relationships. It is important culturally because a society composed of empathetic people is demonstrably more humane than a society comprised of antisocial and narcissistic personalities. Racists, misogynists, and homophobes are what they are partly because they have a limited ability to walk in another person's shoes. Researchers talk about emotional empathy, the ability to feel what another person is feeling, and cognitive empathy, the ability to accurately comprehend what another person is thinking and feeling. They also tell us that empathy starts by developing healthy childhood bonds with parents and caregivers. It is strengthened through education, self-awareness, and practice. Neurological science informs us that empathy can be learned and, when that happens, it creates new pathways in the brain that give us an enhanced ability to enter into relationship with people who are different.

My belief is that Michael Anderson's antisocial behavior was the result of his failure to develop the normal capacity for empathy as a child. His early life of crime exemplifies why society should prioritize the emotional and developmental needs of infants and young people. Fortunately, there is evidence that people can cultivate empathy through therapy, including cognitive behavioral therapy and psychoanalysis. "Compassion therapy," based on Buddhist and Western approaches to building empathy in damaged people, is also a developing strategy for reducing crime and criminal recidivism.

In Michael's case, religious conversion sparked a new way of understanding people and relationships. He learned empathy through prayer augmented by lots of hard work and psychotherapy.

I don't know if Judge Knight ever acknowledged or addressed his own deficits. I hope he did, but I suspect not because he seemed convinced he had risen to high power due to the natural, incontestable order of things. He thought himself a superior person and therefore a logical person to enforce the status quo and protect good people from lesser humans. Of course, it is conceivable I have overstated Judge Knight's dark side. After all, he was a product of his time and culture, not an outlier. His prejudices and self-possession reflected a way of being that characterized many older white American males. Just as I thought him to be arrogant and racist, I imagine he perceived me to be, at age twenty-nine, colossally smug, big-headed, and disrespectful. Michael Anderson's life is rich in lessons about overcoming one's lower nature. He was able to do so in a very tough environment, and it is certainly possible that Judge Knight, in less cruel circumstances, also became more compassionate and forgiving as he aged.

If I am at all empathetic, I owe it to two sources: my parents and my role as a lawyer in resolving legal disputes. My childhood was filled with people of different colors, religions, levels of education, lifestyles, and income. My parents did not expose their children to diversity for the sake of what would now be called political correctness; they did it because it created a fun, stimulating, and rich environment. They marched for civil rights because they liked people of different races and they believed in racial equality. They interacted with poor and less educated people as easily as they mingled with affluent professionals.

Some family experiences were less welcome than others. For instance, I hated the smell of a particular babysitter's dilapidated shack, and I was confused by and afraid of the clear plastic tarp that divided the shack into two rooms, rooms I called "half houses." But Daisy and Bill, the owners of the shack, were Dad's clients. He liked them, sympathized with their impoverished circumstances, and was happy to allow them to pay down their legal fees by babysitting. One summer my parents signed me up to tutor low-income kids at a local nonprofit program. I resisted but was not given a choice in the matter. The experience introduced me to people and cultures I would not have encountered in my routine social circles. My parents' church congregation was diverse and progressive. It included a group of eccentric individuals who were sometimes quirky to the extreme. I was expected to interact with odd individuals at weekly services and church events.

None of this hurt me, although I sometimes felt my autonomy was violated. As I grew older, I learned to appreciate and value exposure to a broad range of people and to differences in wealth and opportunity. These experiences and lessons informed the manner in which my wife and I tried to promote empathy in our own daughter.

Over forty years of lawyering has convinced me that the better lawyers are those whose capacity for empathy enables them to understand clients, opposing parties, and divisive viewpoints. Empathy is central to finding common ground so that disputes can be settled without expensive, protracted, and painful litigation. It is also essential for effective advocacy in the courtroom where lawyers need to accurately communicate a client's perspective while also considering how the world looks through the eyes of witnesses, judges, and jurors. Lawyers who can solve problems efficiently and inexpensively are lawyers who can relate to the concerns and feelings of everyone involved in the dispute, not just their clients. My own professional life has been instructive.

In 1995, about the time Michael was unwrapping his psyche's dark mysteries, I agreed to represent a Gypsy woman who was indicted by a federal grand jury for conspiracy to obstruct justice. She allegedly tried to influence the testimony of certain other members of the Spokane Gypsy community who were government witnesses in a local civil rights case. Co-defendants charged in the case were my client's husband, children, and relatives. The alleged targets of the obstruction were also relatives. The formal accusation could be described as rationale, in my view, only if one assumed the Gypsy community conducted its affairs like local white Presbyterians. In fact, the Gypsy culture in Spokane was a fascinating mix of religious and cultural practices dating back centuries to the migration of the Roma people from the Indian subcontinent to Eastern Europe and the Balkans and, in time, to Western Europe, the United Kingdom, and North America. These practices frequently developed to ensure economic and cultural survival in societies dominated by alien and hostile attitudes. Even today, Gypsies continue to be hectored by the "tramps and thieves" stereotype noted in Cher's famous lyric.

After weeks of studying how Gypsy families operate within the larger Gypsy community, I discovered there was a veiled but powerful system of rules and dogma that underpinned Gypsy culture. This included the customary sophisticated way Gypsies resolved disagreements between and among individuals and families. There was an established hierarchy of leaders and elders. And, importantly, religious tradition mandated rituals and practices that prevented Gypsies from being contaminated by non-Gypsy people. Federal prosecutors either had no understanding of this or considered it so deviant that it was undeserving of deference and respect.

When the case came to trial, the other defense lawyers and I went to great lengths to educate the judge and jury about these matters. We argued that this very prosecution was an example of governmental action designed to punish people who did not embrace mainstream lifestyles and belief systems. The jurors, like most people in eastern Washington, no doubt started the trial with a presumption that the alleged conspirators, including my client, were guilty. Gradually, witness by witness, document by document, historical fact by historical fact, and emotion by emotion, we built a case and invited jurors to enter the world of Spokane Gypsies—a proud people who lived on society's margins, solved their own problems, and daily suffered the condemnatory gaze of white, Christian people who frequently and wrongly believed all Gypsies came from Romania. We won this case because the lawyers immersed themselves in Gypsy customs and history and attitudes. We learned about our Gypsy clients so that we could teach the trial judge and jury to put themselves in the shoes of our clients. The experience has served as a continuing life lesson about the importance of empathy.

Another learning experience—one relating to Mormons—grew out of my work as a law professor. The Mormon religion has fascinated me since

PART 6: EMPATHY AND FAITH

I first heard my father talk about Latter Day Saints when I was young. Dad had grown up in Salt Lake City but was not Mormon. He was a generous and forgiving man who tried to find the good in everyone. He was, in today's parlance, a progressive. This manifested both as an intellectual article of faith and in the tolerant way he treated people of diverse backgrounds and opinions. However, he was conceivably less charitable in his judgment of the LDS religion, if not individual Mormons. He confessed to having felt somewhat marginalized growing up as a "gentile" (his word) in Mormon country. He considered Mormon religious doctrine to be very odd. Of course, every religion is odd, depending on your belief system, and it struck me as ironic that dad never judged, say, the Seventh Day Adventist religion, or Hinduism, the way he judged the LDS Church.

My own understanding of Mormon doctrine leads me to the put the religion on par with Scientology in respect to discussion about planets, disappearing gold tablets, levels of heaven, celestial marriage, race, apostacy, hierarchy, and attitudes toward women. I was once on a ferry from Washington state to Juneau, Alaska, and got buttonholed by a Mormon proselytizer who acted like his one mission in life was to convert me. To get him to stop, I finally told him I was gay and attracted to him.

Given my father's bias and my own intellectual reservations, it is fair to say I was less than empathic when it came to the Mormon Church. Fortunately, my experience as a law professor gave me exposure to Mormon students over several decades. I also had a few Mormon acquaintances and, as a lawyer, I had represented Mormon clients and interacted with Mormon lawyers. I learned something about these folks as individuals and their relationship to their church. I learned about the Mormon community's commitment to the well-being of its members and its emphasis on civility, hard work, and discipline. Even though I would not have voted for Mitt Romney for president, I would trust his work ethic and ability to engage in civilized debate. The Mormons I knew, especially my students, of which there were many, mostly from Utah, could unfailingly be relied upon to work hard, meet deadlines, and treat people with respect and kindness. I didn't have to worry about them spending the night at the local pub when they should have been preparing a brief. Maybe the Church forms these traits in Mormon young people or maybe these traits are already a part of the makeup of those who are drawn to the Church. Either way, knowing them has made me less judgmental of a religion—however bizarre its doctrine—and more appreciative of its followers.

Chapter 31

Parole board member: *"Are you [sorry for what you did]?"*

Red: *"There's not a day goes by I don't feel regret. Not because I'm in here or because you think I should. I look back on the way I was then: A young, stupid kid who committed a terrible crime. I want to talk to him. I want to try and talk some sense to him, tell him the way things are. But I can't. That kid's long gone and this old man is all that's left. I gotta live with that."*

—Shawshank Redemption

The early spring air in eastern Washington was cool, but the sun was out, and the indigo sky covered the scabland like a deep blue dome. As I approached the Coyote Ridge Correctional Center from the north, I was not seized by the melancholia that typically dominates my prison visits. I was optimistic and looking forward to appearing with Michael before the parole board. It was March 20, 2018, almost forty years after Michael had escaped from the Franklin County Jail and terrorized the Carlson family. I was probably overprepared for the hearing and would need to carefully pick and pursue arguments that mattered.

Parole hearings in Washington are informal opportunities to discuss an inmate's progress and decide what sentencing adjustments to make, if any. In Michael's case, two female members of the board were scheduled to meet with Michael, his assigned counselor, and me. The board members were experienced criminal justice professionals who had handled hundreds of parole hearings. Both were sex offense specialists. Unlike formal courtroom proceedings, my role and level of participation were up to the discretion of the board member charged with running the meeting.

If allowed to speak, I was prepared to talk in detail about Michael's early life, what he was like when I first met him, about his extraordinary transformation in 1990, decades of unbroken good behavior, his commitment to psychotherapy, a stellar work history, positive relations with other inmates and prison staff, and a family who had stuck with him. I would

PART 6: EMPATHY AND FAITH

quote passages from favorable psychological evaluations attesting to the fact that Michael was neither a psychopath nor sexually deviant. He had been antisocial during his early life, but his antisocial impulses ended years ago. He had worked successfully, for decades, with men and women in various prison work settings, including both health and food service. Since 1991, there was no evidence of any kind that Michael had committed theft or assault. There was no record of drug use or drug distribution. He had committed no sex offenses and had never been implicated in any kind of sexual conduct, homosexual or otherwise, consensual or coercive.

I hoped also to describe Michael's parole plan—his desire to live with Dee in Spokane, start a commercial custodial services business, and develop a ministry for at-risk young people.

I believed the primary obstacle to Michael's release was an unspoken but powerful reluctance to free a prisoner, even a model inmate like Michael, who had not participated successfully in every conceivable prison program designed to reduce and control hurtful behavior. The Department of Corrections was supposed to keep the public safe. The parole board undoubtedly took that charge seriously, but it also took seriously the goal of not embarrassing the corrections system or provoking political blowback by paroling someone who presented even the slightest risk. This would be especially true where several judicial officers had recommended the inmate never be released. Parole board members did not explicitly say it, but they wanted assurance the chance of recidivism in Michael's case was zero. For that reason, I focused my preparation on research and statistics that correlate aging and criminal recidivism.

Recidivism has been studied for generations. It has been looked at in relation to the nature of the offense, the severity of sentence, the age of the perpetrator at the time of the crime, the presence or absence of family and community support, the age of the inmate on the date of release, and the kind of programming the inmate participated in while incarcerated. Our common sense and experience tell us that offenders age out of criminal behavior. Repeated studies show this to be manifestly and demonstrably true. The reality is that, overall, sixty-five-year-old men who have spent most of their adult lives in prison do not reoffend when released. In fact, the incidence of reoffending as an inmate approaches age seventy is virtually zero. This is true for violent offenders as well as perpetrators of drug and property crimes. I would present data, including statistics assembled in and by the State of Washington, that predicted Michael to be extremely low risk for reoffending. I would argue that the published data on all inmates, including violent offenders and sex offenders, was favorable to Michael even if he had never been married, never had a prison job, never obtained two associate of arts degrees, and never dedicated his life to Christ. The fact that he had done all these things, and more, positioned him, in my view, at the very top of the list of offenders who merit release.

The two female board members were at the reception area when I entered the prison visiting entrance. We all went through security together and the women chatted amiably with me as we waited to be escorted to the office where the hearing would take place. We chatted about families, children, and the vernal equinox. I was relaxed but earnest. I tried to control my optimism about the prospect of Michael being released any time soon. These women seemed intelligent and experienced and might very well give Michael the benefit of the doubt notwithstanding the nature and number of his offenses, and the recommendation of sentencing judges. We assembled in a small, beige-colored room with a rectangular table. There were three chairs on either side. On one side sat Michael, his prison counselor, and me. On the other, the two board members. The room was otherwise bereft of decoration, color, or any hint of the outside world.

Once the hearing got started, the board members were all business. They were surprisingly resolute in their desire to focus the hearing on Michael's two sex offenses that occurred over forty years prior. They asked the same questions counselors and psychologists had asked Michael over and over for decades. "Why did you attack Mrs. Carlson? What were you feeling at the time? How did you feel when the incident was over? What makes you think those same impulses are no longer part of your life?"

Michael answered the questions as best he could and shared not only his memory of the incidents but the process that allowed him to come to terms with his behavior years later. The board members did not want to leave the topic. They inquired about Michael's interest in participating in a yearlong intensive sex offense treatment program before he was paroled. Additionally, even though he had been drug-free for thirty years, the board members asked his opinion about the desirability of participating in an intensive drug treatment program. I had not yet talked and was troubled that the board spent an inordinate amount of time talking about decades-old sex offenses and drug use rather than Michael's decades-long, dedicated work at changing his thoughts, his relationships, his religious orientation, and his heart. Among other things, I was impatient to remind the board that, in four decades, no counselor, therapist, or psychologist had ever identified Michael with sexual deviance or a paraphilic sexual disorder.

I kept my mouth shut while Michael calmly and honestly responded to the board's questions. I was convinced Michael should be released as soon as possible without being required to jump through more hoops. Michael, on the other hand, had grown to see the parole board as part of a divine plan and agency that had helped him chart a course from darkness to a blessed life. What he told the board members was not something he had worked out with a clever lawyer; it was emotionally and spiritually true for him. Michael explained that he did not believe he needed sex offender treatment or substance abuse counseling, but he would welcome such programming if the board, in its discretion and wisdom, believed such treatment was appropriate.

Finally, the board let me speak, and I presented a crisp and solid summary of the data that show older offenders Michael's age are at very low risk of reoffending when released. I talked about Dee's support, the support of prison administrators, the favorable diagnoses of several psychologists, and Michael's hope to give back to society by ministering to young men whose early lives mirrored Michael's own. The presentation included statistical data about divorce in society in general and for prisoners in particular. The divorce rate among all American couples is almost 50 percent. For couples where one spouse is incarcerated for one year or more, the rate is 80 percent for men and close to 100 percent for women. According to one study, each year of incarceration increases the odds that an inmate's marriage will end in divorce by an average of 32 percent. That does not leave many couples in this situation with much hope of making their marriage work. The fact that Michael and Dee had stayed married, strengthened their marriage, and had children, grandchildren, and great-grandchildren while Michael was locked up is not only statistically anomalous, it is a virtual miracle.

Given the informal nature of the hearing, I was able to communicate my long association with Michael, and my work over the years with other convicted criminals who had received lesser sentences for arguably more serious crimes like murder. I shared my personal conviction that there was a moral obligation to let Michael spend his old age outside prison walls. I challenged the board to articulate any possible rationale for keeping Michael in prison for any substantial additional amount of time. What more could he do to demonstrate rehabilitation? How could correctional officers and parole board members be anything but pleased with an inmate whose life at age sixty-five modeled the very change people had hoped for and encouraged? As a child, Michael was the poster boy for potential trouble. As a senior citizen, he represented the kind of success that correctional bureaucrats should want to celebrate.

A few weeks later, we received the board's written decision. It informed Anderson that he would be required to participate in the Sexual Offender Treatment and Assessment Program and a chemical dependence program prior to release. This meant Michael would need to be transferred to another correctional facility—probably the Airway Heights facility, where he had already spent fifteen years. He would be expected to enroll in a year-long program designed to alter the thinking and behavior of inmates who were thirty and forty years younger than Michael and still at risk for reoffending. The decision was not lacking in encouragement, however. First, the board's written decision quoted the findings of a state psychologist who had evaluated Michael's progress and risk factors: "I find Mr. Anderson to be a professional, mature, stable, focused, hard-working, practical, patient and adaptive individual . . . [H]e exemplifies that rehabilitation is possible." Second, board members explicitly acknowledged Michael's spiritual devotion as an authentic and enduring factor in his decades-long commitment to a new life. This was a departure from the board's customary reluctance to comment on a prisoner's religious good faith. Third, the board scheduled another hearing in six months to redetermine Michael's minimum term. This action was not required by law—it signaled the board's readiness to advance Michael's earliest possible release date from 2025 to some earlier date.

Still, I was disappointed and mystified at the board's decision. I thought there was a good chance Michael might be paroled sometime very soon without the necessity of further programming or other conditions. In contrast, Michael accepted the decision without question, saw it all as part of God's plan, and turned his attention to doing what was necessary to facilitate his transfer to Airway Heights so that he could successfully complete the recommended programs.

The Department of Corrections transferred Michael to Airway Heights in November 2018. Before the transfer, the parole board met with him, as promised. It was September 18, Yom Kippur, the Day of Atonement, a day of special meaning to Michael and one that gave him confidence in the Lord's presence. Indeed, the board's decision on that date adjusted Michael's parole eligibility date from 2025 to August 2021. If all went well, Michael would be paroled around his sixty-eighth birthday. And, if Michael successfully completed the one-year sex offense and chemical dependency programs, he could ask the board to accelerate his release to sometime in 2020, when he would be a spry sixty-seven years old. Michael was getting on in life. Fortunately, the criminal justice system was showing signs of looking at the reality of his life, not just the recommendations of judges whose knowledge of Michael was limited to who he was at age twenty-five.

* * * *

The Airway Heights prison is only a fifteen-minute drive from Spokane and Michael's residence there affords me the opportunity to see him regularly. Our visits take place in a small unadorned beige room surrounded by prison guards, thick walls, and razor wire. Michael's aging body is still locked up, but his mind and spirit have long since been liberated. His interests range from the pedestrian to the sublime. Our conversations are upbeat and forward looking. It is easy to understand how he is a source of inspiration for fellow inmates, his mother, and for his devoted wife, three children, sixteen grandchildren, and five great-grandchildren. Michael believes his participation in his treatment program is a blessing because it gives him valuable insights he can use after his parole in dealing with the range of issues that affect young at-risk men on the streets. Michael is endlessly curious, and he does not cease to surprise me—not least when he recounts an anecdote or story, something that usually took place in the context of his programming, that enables him to better understand who he was as a child, adolescent, or a young adult. That there is something to learn every day is not just a trite aphorism for Michael. His world is a place of learning, of expectation, and hope.

The year 2019 went by quickly as we waited for Michael to finish his program and move towards scheduling a new board hearing. He treasured his regular visits with his wife, of course, and those occasions when his children and grandchildren were able to see him. It appeared to me, however, that he was most moved by the opportunity to see his aging mother.

Abigail had always tried to see Michael every few years since he first went to the penitentiary. These visits were important to Michael, but they became especially important once he matured and started to gain perspective and understanding about his childhood, and what he had missed. Prior to 2019, Abigail had last visited in 2017. Her journey to visit him and Dee in June 2019, to celebrate Michael's sixty-sixth birthday, was an event of incalculable emotional significance. They had three days of laughter, reminiscing, and joy. Abigail was physically frail, with a weak heart, and her travel by air from Chicago to Spokane was a real hardship. Michael knew she would not be able to travel much longer. He appreciated her sacrifice because he knew this visit might be their last opportunity to speak and demonstrate matters of the heart. Their relationship had long since moved beyond the point of acknowledging the unmet needs of a wounded little boy and his damaged mother. Both knew the past was the past, but they wholeheartedly committed themselves to living in the present in a way that intentionally counteracted the meager emotional nourishment of those early days. They regularly communicated their love and support for one another by letter and telephone.

Their parting in June was emotional and sublime. Michael and Dee knew they would not likely see Abigail again, but they also knew they would always be together in Christ and that it would be just a matter of time before they would all be together on the other side. Michael told his mother he loved her, and she responded: "I love you, too, Michael, and always will."

I had the pleasure of spending an evening with Abigail during her June 2019 visit. She moved slowly, painfully, a relic of what I imagined her to be in her early days. But her mind was clear, and I was grateful she agreed to reminisce about her life and family even though the effort opened unhappy wounds for a mother burdened by the knowledge that a son she loved had spent most of his life in prison. She ate like a bird as she chatted with my wife and me over dinner about Michael's youth and descent into darkness. The conversation was interrupted periodically while Abigail paused to remember and describe a young black mother's struggle to survive in an era that predated modern civil rights law, good jobs for black women, economic independence from men, and birth control.

Abigail died on October 31, 2019 in Massachusetts, in the care of her daughter. She was eighty-nine years old and had gotten weaker and weaker after visiting Michael and Dee. Michael was overcome once more with guilt that the family's eldest son could not be there to shepherd his mother through her suffering. He had prayed for her return to good health and talked to her every day by phone. Finally, when it was clear Abigail's pain would not subside, he prayed and asked the Lord to end her physical agony and let her go.

PART 6: EMPATHY AND FAITH

Just before she died, Michael telephoned his mother to say that he imagined himself to be like Rebekah's beloved son, Jacob. As told in the book of Genesis, Jacob (later to be known as Israel) was touched by God after seeking his blessing and wrestling with an angel while returning to his home in Canaan following a long absence in a foreign land. Soon thereafter, Rachel, his much-loved wife, died at the gates of Bethlehem. Michael, too, had been touched by God after a long struggle and, like Jacob, he lost a beloved family member as he neared the celebration of his homecoming.

Chapter 32

*"Blessed are the peacemakers, for they will
be called children of God."*

—MATTHEW 5:9

Many prisoners have privately owned television sets in their cells. Michael considers television a distraction and has not had one since 1997. He has no access to the internet and limited access to outgoing telephone calls. He cannot receive incoming calls. He has never voted, never marched, never attended a city council meeting, taught Sunday school, or worshipped in a cathedral. His religion is based on doctrinal evangelical teachings, but it is intensely private, personal, and spiritual. In many ways, his faith has been practiced and nurtured in the manner of the monastic—separated from the world and removed from its secular and religious strife.

I do not know how it works, but I don't doubt religion's capacity to produce meaningful and beneficial change in individuals. Something happens, though, when faith jumps from an individual's spiritual search for meaning to an established organization's need to proselytize, convert, and control. History teaches us to be skeptical when faith is organized into hardened doctrine, associated with infallible sacred texts, and elaborated through layers of rules, expectations, and governing systems. Once imbedded as a source of political and cultural power, the public face of private devotion will almost certainly aspire to increase its power. How could it not? It has all the answers for both this life and the next. Thus, religion becomes tribal and is susceptible to Machiavellian political alliances, xenophobia, and aggression.

Disagreement among non-believers or believers of alternative faiths unfortunately provokes more than just interesting and stimulating debate. It can produce war, intolerance, inequity, and cultural divisions that stand as historical contradictions to what one might expect after studying the essential teachings of prophets, wise men, gurus, saints, popes, pujari, priests, imams, rabbis, and shamans. We are all too familiar with the historical examples where religious, racial, and political differences produced volatile and horrific outcomes.

Like many Christians and non-Christians, I have difficulty condemning to eternal damnation the souls of billions of Jews, Muslims, Hindu, Buddhists, and others, living and dead, simply because they failed to understand—or had no opportunity to understand—that salvation requires acceptance of Jesus as a personal savior. I am not persuaded that the incontestable and literal word of God is contained in writings collected by competing clerics hundreds of years after the time Jesus walked the paths of Galilee, Samaria, and Judaea.

The major Western monotheist religions developed at different times, but all in the Middle East, and all with a common pedigree in sacred ancient stories. If you hope to understand God and God's plan in the Western world, it is likely the Abrahamic narratives will influence you. We might imagine this would have led to an integrated and congenial mix of like-minded people and cultures. It did not. The common narratives took different turns on their way to becoming alternative versions of the truth. Those competing truths have in common the bedrock ideals of love and compassion. They have also engendered hatred and violence and intolerance.

Pope Urban II was famously known for his speech in Clermont, France, in 1095 that exhorted church leaders, noblemen, and commoners to free Jerusalem from control of the infidels. "When an armed attack is made upon the enemy, let this one cry be raised by all the soldiers of God: It is the will of God!" In March 2019, a New Zealand man posted a manifesto that echoed Pope Urban II's call for Christian crusades against Muslims. The man then entered two mosques during prayer and murdered fifty worshipers while livestreaming his attack on Facebook. A few weeks later, a half a world away in Sri Lanka, several Muslims strapped bombs to their backs and blew up hundreds of Christians attending Easter church services or eating Easter breakfast at luxury hotels.

I am not learned in the all details and differences that distinguish the Abrahamic narratives, but I cannot stop wondering when we will be released from their jealous and divisive grip. I imagine some magical time when all religion merges into undifferentiated unity, and we worship a divinity whose perfect embrace encompasses all gods and the imperfection of humankind.

* * * *

How does this relate to Michael? I wonder, if he is released from his enforced monasticism, how the modern American and global cultural wars will affect him. Will his attention turn from washing and feeding the sick and the dying to taking up metaphorical arms in the fight against secular society? Can he avoid being sucked into the vortex of digital meanness? Will the powerful forces at work in the evangelical world compel him to make heroes of people who seek to divide, exclude, punish, and demean? Will he profess the biblical certainty and inevitability of the End of Times as a justification for doing nothing about environmental degradation and interminable war?

I am mindful of the fact that the experience of evangelical conversion for African Americans arose, paradoxically, in the context of slavery where religion was used as a justification to oppress people. The notion that slavery was good because it delivered a pagan people to a Christian culture held sway for centuries despite the utter hypocrisy and self-serving nature of the claim. Nonetheless, as Howard Thurman said in his book, *Deep River*, something positive came out of slave religion in America. "By some amazing but vastly creative spiritual insight the slave undertook the redemption of a religion that the master had profaned in his midst." I am hopeful that Michael's Christian conversion is best understood as a product of this historic struggle for spiritual salvation and bodily freedom.

I have spent a good deal of time teaching and consulting in the Middle East, including the Holy Land, and one evening, sitting on my terrace in Ramallah, in the West Bank, just outside of Jerusalem, I wrote:

> *Twilight turns this dirt where Jesus walked*
> *into the October innocence of a Fall night*
> *on the Columbia River Plateau, after harvest,*
> *when I was young.*
>
> *I sing of blood and rocks and dirt,*
> *the horizon connected by a thread to my blood,*
> *the blood infused by all that I hope to know and forget, the blood of*
> *this land and my land and all land.*
>
> *You can fall into Ramallah from Israel as into a dream*
> *from which there is no exit.*
> *You dream things more noble than barbed wire,*
> *things that move the heart from shame to holiness.*

PART 6: EMPATHY AND FAITH

Our fears are nurtured in dark places where imagination is dead.

But see that distant glow?
It cuts the night and beckons.
Broken and homesick, we might crawl,
painfully,

And stir the embers of our love.

Having all this in mind, I one day put an ecclesiastical question to Michael. It laid out the age-old conundrum for those seeking to compare and understand various faith traditions. I did not expect a definitive answer. On the other hand, it was not a trick question and I did not mean it rhetorically. Here is what I wrote to Michael:

There are plenty of people who are kind, virtuous, and unselfish without any faith commitment, Christian or otherwise. There are also millions of good people who are guided by beliefs that developed in other religious or philosophical traditions. For instance, the Dali Lama (by all accounts) is as Christlike or more Christlike than most Christians. He professes, like Christ, a philosophy of love, compassion, and forgiveness. And yet he, the Dali Lama, is a dedicated Buddhist who does not preach the Bible's literal meaning or the proposition that Jesus is the only path to God and enlightenment. How does this square with your understanding of the role Christ plays in the world?

Michael's response was characteristically humble but assured:

Just like the fall came by one man, salvation came by one man. The Dalai Lama, Buddha, and Mohammed were all great human beings but, with all due respect, none of them conquered hell, death, and the grave. Many people are good people, but they cannot be Christlike unless they have invited Christ into their lives. People, even good people, will always be troubled. Sin is in our nature. Christ does not take that away. Instead, he shows us a new way, we learn to hear and follow his voice, we learn to wait for him, to trust him, and to love him. I do not know how the Lord *is going to get his family out of the earth, that is much too complicated for me. But I do know that I must work on my own salvation with fear and trembling. I have studied myself to be approved of God a workman, who need not be ashamed, rightly dividing the word of truth. I have forged a relationship with my creator who has made himself real to me. The evidence is in the freedom that I have, the peace that I have, the confidence that I have, and the certainty that I can and will contribute to humanity. This he has promised me.*

I was tempted to pursue this dialogue. I was curious, for example, to find out how Michael comprehends the difference between the Beast, the Anti-Christ, and Satan. I wanted to know why Nazi butchers might be admitted into heaven by embracing Jesus on their death bed, while the Jewish babies they slaughtered would be exiled from God's presence for eternity. But while I am entertained and stimulated by efforts to pierce religious mystery with intellectual inquiry, I really have no desire to debate Michael on his understanding of Christianity. My reasons? Michael's relationship with God is real whether or not God is the transcendent power represented in the Bible. I have no business questioning a belief system that has done so much to transform and redeem a life that was considered unsalvageable. Also, Michael's relationship with me is real, and I don't want to interpose between us a barrier constructed of religious imponderables and straw men.

I do not know if religious conviction should be explained by reference to the divine or by conventional psychology. However, I support it wholeheartedly when it works. My effort to understand and describe Michael's life leaves me with a deeper appreciation for the power of religious healing. My resistance to religion, if any, has nothing to do with the individual soul. It is a reaction to organized ways of thinking about God that mutate into justifications for hurting and diminishing other humans or wounding the earth.

If God's message to humanity is one of love and compassion, can an individual's spiritual journey avoid entanglement with doctrinal and institutional forces that undermine that message?

Many years ago, I read a book by John Fowles, *The Magus*, that contains a wonderfully described vignette about a blind man who lived alone on the edge of a fiord in the far reaches of Norway's vast northern wilderness. The man was a hermit and seemingly misanthropic if not completely insane. Upon close observation, it became evident that the man lived in relationship with God and maintained an eccentric lifestyle that allowed nothing to come between them. At night, the man would walk under the northern lights to the edge of the sea where he would call out in a voice that echoed across the firth: "I am waiting" or "I am here." The man was not, in fact, always waiting. He spent his nights in the company of God and there was no distracting voice or canonical prescription that told him his communion was wrong.

I imagine the scene almost thirty years ago when Michael was alone in his cell and a man came by to tell him all he had to do was believe. He was not in a megachurch and he had no Bible, no internet, and no one to tell him what to believe, who to believe, or who to fear. His relationship with God started in an almost romantic way, a way that probably appeals to Christian and other religious sects that disavow dogma and hierarchy. I like to think the same experience might be accessible to anyone—in a prison cell or a palace—in Saudi Arabia, China, Sri Lanka, Sudan, New Zealand, North Korea, or America.

* * * *

While I do not wish to pursue debate with Michael on the basic tenents of his faith, there are other questions that I have felt very comfortable pursuing with him. Why couldn't the young Michael see and accept God? How do the dark forces in one's life prevent us from seeing and living in the light? Are some people born into circumstances that invite darkness and confusion while others are blessed with the conditions that favor the light?

Michael's early life was a virtual laboratory for exploring these questions and he is enthusiastic in sharing his wisdom. I asked him to describe what he remembers about the darkness. His answer is not especially surprising, but his subsequent comments about what prison has meant to him are revealing:

> *You learn in the darkness to conceal, to deny the truth. There is no peace in the darkness, no rest, no comfort. This is why so many people become so weary and they forfeit their lives to suicide. I have seen many men take their own lives to escape. The darkness has no mercy. It does not discriminate—it is an equal opportunity employer. Your will, your intellect, your emotions, your memory, your imagination are prime targets of the darkness. Its sole intention is to steal, kill, and destroy. Pessimism is a product of darkness. It gives you a fatalistic outlook, your thinking is horribly flawed, your logic is fictitious, so you take chances with no respect for consequences. Yes, the darkness is our greatest adversary. The depths of depravity are found only in darkness. It is a phenomenon that paralyzes its victims—it has the ability to transform the human composition to predatory, animal-like behavior. You develop a preoccupation with physical desires and selfish desires regardless of the cost to others. The darkness overwhelms ordinary conscience and intuition. Unrestrained impulses and emotions propel you further and further into a place of total isolation where logic and reason are rendered powerless.*

When darkness is exposed in our lives, it is extremely painful. The humiliation, the shame, the regret is overwhelming when we finally see the destruction, the devastation, and mayhem we have left in our wake. We become perplexed and confused as to how we could lend ourselves to such pathetic endeavors. I see many men, including myself, cry like little children once they have an opportunity to reflect, to ponder the acts committed in the darkness. The radio, the television, the newspaper, the internet all testify to deeds we never expected to be exposed.

I am so grateful for prison. I can see why the one who created everything commanded his people to visit the prisoners. Prison gives you the opportunity to reflect, to contemplate, to analyze, to reason. Eventually you have to take a look at yourself. There is nowhere to run, to hide. You get tired of lying to yourself, blaming others, and always coming up on the short end of the stick. I was blessed to escape the darkness before it could fulfill its intentions, but I was its hostage for the better part of thirty-seven years.

Epilogue

> *"One of every seven people in prison in the United States—a total of more than two hundred thousand people—is currently serving a life prison term, more than the entire prison population in 1972, before the advent of mass incarceration."*
>
> —Marc Mauer and Ashley Nellis, *The Meaning of Life*

> *"48% of people serving life or 'virtual life' prison sentences are African American and another 15% are Latino."*
>
> —U.S. Bureau of Justice Statistics, *Prisoners in 2016*, (Jan. 2018)

Michael's attitude about being black in American society is not something he talks about easily. His preoccupation and emphasis at age sixty-six relates to his relationship with Jesus and his decades-long commitment to living a righteous and pious life.

But as a white man and a white writer, especially as a writer who aspires to capture parts of a story that can only be accessed indirectly and vicariously, there is an element to Michael's childhood that intrigues me. My early education about the black experience in America came from the good fortune of having teachers and professors who required me to read books like *The Invisible Man* (Ralph Ellison), *Native Son* (Richard Wright), *The Fire Next Time* (James Baldwin), and *Black Like Me* (John Howard Griffin). I learned about slavery and being black by reading Frederick Douglass, Booker T. Washington, W. E. B. DuBois, and Langston Hughes; and, later, from writers and poets and professionals and academics, like Maya Angelou, Toni Morrison, Thurgood Marshall, and Cornel West. Of course, movies, especially those directed by Spike Lee, helped me understand nuances in African American culture that I could never experience directly. And I loved Dick Gregory and Richard Pryor, who taught me to understand racial prejudice by learning to laugh at myself and the worldview I had inherited by growing up white and privileged. My point is that I was influenced about the black experience even though I did not live it, and even though Michael Anderson does not interpret his life primarily through the lens of race.

As I grappled with how to portray Michael's early life in this book, I, of course, shared periodic drafts of my writing with Michael. A slight tension soon crept into our communication around the question of how to portray his mother and stepfather. My inclination was to describe Michael as a victim of abuse and neglect and chaos. Indeed, the book reflects, at least in part, that Michael suffered a traumatic early life as a result of parental shortcomings. From time to time, however, Michael would push back and suggest that the portraits of Abigail and Andy needed to be softened and enhanced. I was skeptical, because I assumed Michael was asking me to sanitize his early family life and compromise the story's integrity. But our conversations became more nuanced. Michael repeatedly reminded me that the family situation was more complex, that there was another layer, something that had to do with Abigail's and Andy's efforts to protect him from the consequences of bad decisions. Michael was telling me that it was an oversimplification to describe Andy simply as a drunken, insensitive child abuser.

Thus, I want to look at the possibility that Michael's parents were greatly concerned about Michael throwing himself against the world in a way that was bound to attract the negative attention of law enforcement, public officials, and society in general. While they were largely inadequate in expressing affection and communicating feelings, and while their disciplinary methods were sometimes cruel, did Andy and Abigail see their primary parental role as one of protecting Michael from himself, and preparing him to survive in a harsh and unfair environment? Was their goal, in their broken way, to keep Michael close to home and anchor him to the acceptable norms and boundaries of working-class, urban African American life?

The black playwright August Wilson touches on this theme in his play *Fences* (which is set in the 1950s), through his depiction of the emotional distance that separates a traditional, harsh, and hardworking urban black father and his children who seek independence both from him and from racial restrictions. James Baldwin spoke eloquently of the same issue in a 1962 New Yorker essay, *Letter from a Region of My Mind*, which later became part of his book *The Fire Next Time*. He was writing about the challenges faced by young people and their elders in Harlem in the 1940s:

EPILOGUE

> This world is white, and they are black. White people hold the power . . . and the world has innumerable ways of making this difference known and felt and feared. . . . Every effort made by the child's elders to prepare him for a fate from which they cannot protect him causes him secretly, in terror, to begin to await, without knowing that he is doing so, his mysterious and inexorable punishment. He must be "good" not only in order to please his parents and not only to avoid being punished by them; behind their authority stands another, nameless and impersonal, infinitely harder to please, and bottomlessly cruel. And this filters into the child's consciousness through his parents' tone of voice as he is being exhorted, punished, or loved; in the sudden, uncontrollable note of fear heard in his mother's or his father's voice when he has strayed beyond some boundary. He does not know what the boundary is, and he can get no explanation of it, which is frightening enough, but the fear he hears in the voices of his elders is more frightening still.

Baldwin's comments may or may not inform our understanding of how Michael's mother and stepfather tried to protect him. But I am interested in the notion that black parents, regardless of education or station or parental dysfunction, found it necessary to teach their children about the dangers of crossing lines drawn by tradition and conventions. There is no question that handcuffing a child to a bed frame is abusive, arguably criminal, and ultimately counterproductive. On the other hand, if an unsophisticated parent's goal in the 1950s or 1960s was to keep a young person from pursuing destructive choices, especially choices that might bring down on the child the punitive weight and wrath of white power, perhaps that parent is to be forgiven his or her excesses, or at least assigned a measure of empathy.

Beyond the subject of how black children learn to fear white people, Baldwin, in the same essay, addresses the prospects, including criminal prospects, of a hypothetical low-income urban black child:

> Crime became real, for example—for the first time—not as a possibility but as the possibility. One would never defeat one's circumstances by working and saving one's pennies; one would never, by working, acquire that many pennies, and, besides, the social treatment accorded even the most successful Negroes proved that one needed, in order to be free, something more than a bank account. One needed a handle, a lever, a means of inspiring fear. It was absolutely clear that the police would whip you and take you

in as long as they could get away with it, and that everyone else—housewives, taxi-drivers, elevator boys, dishwashers, bartenders, lawyers, judges, doctors, and grocers—would never, by the operation of any generous human feeling, cease to use you as an outlet for his frustrations and hostilities. Neither civilized reason nor Christian love would cause any of those people to treat you as they presumably wanted to be treated; only the fear of your power to retaliate would cause them to do that, or to seem to do it, which was (and is) good enough.

I am quoting text written sixty years ago, but it resonates for me today, as a white man who has lived through what we now call the "civil rights" era. It resonates because there is still tension throughout the land. From Seattle to Boston to Minneapolis and Baton Rouge, and from Miami to New Orleans and Los Angeles and Chicago and Houston, we are wounded by America's original sin, the curious institution that enabled eighteenth- and nineteenth-century plantation owners to live such charming and abundant lives.

More specifically, I have quoted Baldwin because he has deepened and enlarged my understanding of the cultural dynamics that confronted little Michael when he came into the world in June 1953.

* * * *

Michael Anderson's life is a story of choices—bad choices he made as a young man and good choices he made to get healthy and stay healthy. It is also about choices made by legislators, judges, prosecutors, defense lawyers, parole board members, and others who participate in the criminal justice system. Overlaying all this are issues of race and poverty, cultural attitudes and beliefs about criminal accountability, and the purpose of punishment. This, in turn, implicates our religious and philosophical traditions as well as our scientific understanding of what makes people tick.

Unfortunately, the American approach to criminal justice has created a huge, expensive, and unwieldy crisis in the last thirty or forty years. We have become a nation of mass incarceration and inhumanly long sentences. We jail and imprison more people per capita than any other country, including China, North Korea, Iran, and Saudi Arabia. We spend more money on prisons than any other country. Poor people and people of color are vastly overrepresented in our prison population as compared to their numbers in the general population. The reasons for this are not mysterious. The causes of mass incarceration and long sentences can quickly and easily be identified by looking at laws and procedures enforced in local, state, and federal jurisdictions in the past fifty years. We can trace racial disparities to the effects of slavery and racism that historically infected virtually every important American institution from banking and housing to education, employment, voting, and criminal justice.

Michael Anderson committed heinous offenses. If it is possible to argue that he has spent too much time in prison, imagine the circumstances of a young African American man who never committed a crime of violence but is sentenced to ten or fifteen years in a federal prison—not because a judge or probation officer or psychologist believed he belonged there, but because federal lawmakers made a deal with the devil when they agreed to pass mandatory sentencing laws thirty years ago to show they were *tough on crime* and fully engaged in the *war on drugs*. There are thousands of people in our prisons who are not violent but who cannot be released because of draconian laws. The cost to society is incalculable when you include not only the taxpayer burden but the consequence of taking people away from jobs, spouses, children, and educational opportunities. That some of these people are in prison for distributing marijuana, now a legal substance in many jurisdictions, is ironic, sad, and maddening. As a young lawyer, I represented defendants who were sent to prison for distributing and possessing cannabis. It occurred to me then, and it haunts me now, that the market for the drug that sent many people to prison was incongruously comprised of courthouse officials, businesspeople, college students, and professionals (in addition to less educated and less affluent people who are often identified with drug use). What lesson can we learn from the fact that we used to lock people up, sometimes for years, for selling what today you can buy legally in any city in Washington?

Before going further, I want to speak clearly and directly to readers who believe that mass incarceration of poor people and people of color is explainable by the assumption that these people simply commit more crimes as compared to white and more affluent people. There are dozens of books, articles, and studies that refute this logic. The reality is that law enforcement, courts, and prisons focus on wrongdoers who are the least able to defend themselves in terms of finances, political clout, and social position. Consider a couple of examples.

Example #1: Defendant X is a local businessman, member of the Chamber of Commerce, and churchgoer. He is picked up and arrested on a charge of driving while intoxicated. His breathalyzer test shows blood alcohol content of .18, over twice the legal limit. Defendant X posts bond in the amount of $500, calls his wife, and goes home. In time, he hires a lawyer and works out a deal where he avoids jail time in exchange for alcohol counseling and payment of a substantial fine. He also loses his license for several months. It is a regrettable and embarrassing experience, but, for Defendant X, life goes on. He pays the court fine with savings. His wife drives him to work or he takes an Uber while waiting to get his license back.

Defendant Y is also picked up for driving while intoxicated. His breathalyzer test result is .1, just over the legal limit. Defendant Y is arrested, but he cannot make bail because he is young and unemployed. He owes money to several creditors and his ex-wife. He sits in jail for a few days until he can talk to a public defender and ask a judge for pre-trial release. In the end, he agrees to a plea bargain where he gets a day in jail, with credit for time served, probation, and a substantial fine in addition to loss of his license. He is supposed to pay off his fine by making monthly payments to the court. He misses a few payments and the court issues an order for him to come to court to explain. He misses the court appearance because he has moved and never got notice of the hearing. A warrant is issued, and Defendant Y is picked up and jailed, this time for several days. He finally sees a judge and promises to do better in making his court payments. But Defendant Y cannot keep a job because he has no driver's license. Finally, he decides to drive without a license so that he can get back and forth to a new job at a warehouse. He is picked up for Driving While License Suspended and thrown in jail. He cannot make bail and sits in jail until he can see a judge. The judge revokes his probation on the drunk driving charge and sentences him to thirty days in jail. When he gets out, he will still not have a license and will be expected to resume his court payments or risk further incarceration.

The above example does not explain why state and federal prisons are full, but because the scenario is repeated endlessly in communities throughout the nation, it explains why our local jails are stuffed with people who are essentially being incarcerated because they have no money.

Example #2: Law enforcement in Seattle, King County, Washington is perennially stretched thin in terms of resources that can be focused on drug interdiction. Detectives and patrolmen know that illegal drug use goes on throughout the city and county. Students and professors at the University of Washington smoke grass and snort cocaine. Suburban housewives abuse opioids. People of all colors and ages drink excessively. Young people, intellectuals, spiritual wanderers, and thrill-seekers consume mushrooms, LSD, and other psychedelics. But the jails and prisons are not filled with housewives, college students, intellectuals, or spiritual wanderers. They are filled with young people of color who visibly hang out in targeted neighborhoods and other locations known to police as places they can make easy arrests. There is simply not enough money in the budget, or political will, to bust respectable people in Bellevue or a fraternity house in the University District. The young black kids who get picked up for drug possession or distribution go to jail because they made bad choices, yes, but also because they did not live privileged lives in protected enclaves outside the inner city.

This example is not apocryphal, and it is not exaggerated. In fact, it is based on serious and systematic empirical studies of law enforcement practices in King County in the 1990s. Entitled *The Impact of Race and Ethnicity on Charging and Sentencing Processes for Drug Offenders in Three Counties of Washington State* and *A Study on Racial and Ethnic Disparities in Superior Court Bail and Pre-trial Detention Practices in Washington*, the studies show that if you were young, black, and involved in drugs in downtown Seattle, or in Seattle's dominant black neighborhoods in the Central District, your chances of getting busted were many times greater than if you were a white drug user in another part of town. Among the many statistics produced by the studies was this: although African Americans constituted 3 percent of Washington's overall population, they accounted for 37 percent of the "persistent offender" sentences handed down by Washington courts. These studies were used in a federal lawsuit filed by a colleague of mine at Gonzaga who argued that felon disenfranchisement in Washington was illegal under the Voting Rights Act because racially disparate police, prosecutorial, and judicial practices resulted in a disproportionate number of people of color in Washington prisons. In the course of that litigation, a federal judge found "compelling" evidence of racial discrimination in the Washington criminal justice system.

The current rate of incarceration for African American men nationwide is nearly six times as much as that of their white counterparts. In fact, of the 2.2 million people in the American correctional system, about a million are black—a total that is larger than the entire prison populations of England, Argentina, Canada, and six other countries *combined*. Two-thirds of people serving life sentences in the United States are people of color.

The problem of excessively long-term incarceration requires consideration of sentencing policies that goes beyond giving breaks only to offenders whose crimes are non-violent, non-serious, and nonsexual. Empirical research consistently shows that locking up people for very long periods of time is unnecessary for public safety purposes, and counterproductive in terms of missed life opportunities for the incarcerated. Studies show that people almost always age out of crime, particularly by their late thirties and forties. A person locked up for robbery or murder at age twenty-one is highly unlikely to commit that same crime when he gets out at forty-one. These are statistical norms. If you focus more closely on someone whose institutional history reflects the kind of pro-social growth and commitment to change shown by Michael, the risk is even more negligible.

The data also support changing our responses to some of the crimes that scare people most: people convicted of sexual assault and homicide are actually among the least likely to reoffend after release. People convicted of homicide are the least likely to be rearrested, and those convicted of rape or sexual assault have rearrest rates roughly 30–50 percent lower than people convicted of larceny or motor vehicle theft. More broadly, people convicted of *any* violent offense are less likely to be rearrested in the years after release than those convicted of property, drug, or public order offenses. Yet people convicted of violent offenses often face decades of incarceration, and those convicted of sexual offenses can be committed to indefinite confinement.

The above statistics are taken from a well-researched and thoughtful book on the subject, *The Meaning of Life: The Case for Abolishing Life Sentences*, by Marc Mauer and Ashley Nellis. The authors tell us that the number of people sentenced to prison for life grew from 34,000 in 1984 to *nearly 162,000* in 2016. The United States' attraction to life sentences in the last few decades puts it in a league of its own. Mauer and Nellis explained, "A comprehensive 2016 international analysis of life imprisonment found that the number of people serving life imprisonment in the United States is higher than the *combined* total in the other 113 countries surveyed." Americans are sentenced to life imprisonment at a rate of sixty-four per 100,000, a rate that exceeds the incarceration rate for all categories of sentences in Denmark, Finland, and Sweden.

Policy choices, not criminal offending patterns, drove this dramatic expansion in both the number of people incarcerated in America and the length of their sentences. The "tough on crime" laws that became popular in the 1980s included *enhanced drug violation* penalties, *habitual offender* laws, *three strikes* laws, *and life without possibility of parole* laws, as well as laws that subjected juvenile offenders to adult prison sentences. These laws typically keep people incarcerated even when they no longer pose a threat to public safety. The problem was exacerbated by indeterminate sentencing laws that increasingly allowed judges the discretion to impose a wide sentencing range up to life. This was the case in Washington at the time Michael Anderson was sentenced to multiple consecutive life terms. At least Anderson was fortunate to be sentenced in a jurisdiction that gave a parole board power to someday let him out based on the kind of person he was at age fifty or sixty or seventy and not just based on who he was at age twenty-five when he was initially sentenced. Consider the following egregious case of excessive sentencing in the State of Louisiana, described in the Mauer and Nellis book.

Fate Vincent Winslow, an African American man, was sentenced to life without parole after his fourth non-violent felony conviction. He was convicted of burglaries in 1984 and 1994. In 2004, he was convicted of drug possession. In 2008, he sold twenty dollars' worth of drugs to an undercover police officer. A jury convicted him by a vote of ten to two. The ten votes for conviction were all from white jurors, the two for acquittal were from black jurors. The judge sentenced Winslow to life as a habitual offender. He will be in a Louisiana prison until he dies.

If we are to rethink prison sentences, we need to rethink why we put people in prison. Is it for purely for public safety? If so, the data show that long sentences produce diminishing benefits at enormous cost. Michael Anderson is a good example. He has not hurt anyone—in or out of prison—for decades. But we have kept him locked up at a cost that increased dramatically once he began suffering the medical conditions that tend to afflict aging prisoners. Public safety resources are finite, and correctional budgets devoted to housing and health care for prisoners like Anderson are unavailable to invest in prevention, education, and mental health services. The millions of dollars spent to keep an older low-risk population incarcerated are the result of policies based on emotion and politics, not evidence.

If we put people in prison for revenge, when is revenge enough? At what point did society extract its rightful pound of flesh from Michael Anderson? Is our collective bloodlust so great that we want to continue pouring scarce public dollars into long-term incarceration even though it does not make us safer? Reinvestment of prison savings into programs and strategies that reduce crime is not simply a progressive humanitarian idea, it is a fiscally sound and conservative strategy for an electorate that increasingly wants to see tax dollars used wisely and efficiently.

Norway has a correctional system that looks very kind by US prison standards. Most sentences are capped at twenty years, including crimes of violence. Prison cells are relatively comfortable. Rehabilitation programs are widely available; in fact, inmates are required to have at least one activity in the daytime, whether a job, education, or, say, a sex offender program. Guards are trained, with at least a two-year college requirement, to treat inmates with respect and facilitate their rehabilitation. Norway also has better support once people get out of prison, with a stronger social safety net than the United States—one that includes guarantees for health care and education. Norway has fewer people in prison per capita than the United States at less cost. Its crime rate is also lower.

That's not to say that Norway's prisons are a great place to be. They are unpleasant residences for people who, themselves, may be unpleasant. Inmates still lose almost all their freedoms. They're still taken from their friends, family, and communities. Norwegians do not want to go to Norwegian prisons.

The 2017 Model Penal Code of the American Law Institute concludes that "terms for single offenses in excess of twenty years are rarely justified on proportionality grounds and are too long to serve most utilitarian purposes." Of course, some crimes or offenders should be incarcerated longer, but these would be exceptional cases where there is an individualized diagnosis of mental aberration or dangerousness that necessitates long-term incapacitation.

Mauer and Nellis end their book with a call to American democracy's better angels. "Fundamentally, Americans must ask ourselves what kind of society we wish to live in. Despite the progress we have made, we are nonetheless defined as a nation by centuries of racism, growing inequality, and extreme punishment. Ending life imprisonment would constitute a major step in making us a more just and humane society."

Michael Anderson's journey is not over. He remains in prison hoping and praying to avoid Covid-19 infection in conditions that make it difficult to stay distant from other inmates. The parole board has advanced his release date to June 13, 2021. Some considerable part of the forty-two years he has now been incarcerated was undoubtedly necessary to protect society and to give Michael a meaningful chance at redemption. Few people now would argue that any practical purpose is served by making him die in prison—the goal of the criminal justice system when I first met Michael. When he is released, he may find his new life to be harder to adjust to than he imagined. His faith may be challenged by autonomy, temptations, and frustrations that did not exist in a controlled institutional setting. If so, I have every confidence he will manage and adapt in ways that are considerate of those around him and that show his gratitude and obedience to God. If he could learn and apply those behaviors in the cruel conditions of a state penitentiary, he will surely have success beyond prison walls.

Postscript

Michael has never been able to apologize to the people he terrorized in 1978 because Department of Corrections policy prohibits an offender's contact with crime victims. After checking with corrections officials to make sure that policy is not being violated, he asked that I end the book with these words addressed to people he has hurt:

"The terror that I brought to you in 1978 was unconscionable. I am ashamed of how I betrayed you and my own humanity. I am sure there have been consequences I will never fully comprehend. I subjected you to unquestionable pain and horror. I owe a great debt to you and to society. I cannot change the past, but today and every day to come, I will strive to be the best human I can be. I ask for your forgiveness in that light."

www.ingramcontent.com/pod-product-compliance
Lightning Source LLC
Chambersburg PA
CBHW021731220426
43662CB00008B/804